Play Scratch
GOLF

An Amateur's Guide to Playing Perfect Golf

T0159044

Frederick Fell Publishers, Inc
2131 Hollywood Blvd., Suite 305
Hollywood, Fl 33020
www.Fellpub.com
email: Fellpub@aol.com

Frederick Fell Publishers, Inc
2131 Hollywood Blvd., Suite 305
Hollywood, Fl 33020

First Frederick Fell trade book edition September 2008

For information about special discounts for bulk purchases, Please contact Frederick Fell Special Sales at business@fellpublishers.com.

Designed by Elena Solis

Manufactured in the United States of America

10 9 8 7 6 5 4 3 2 1

Library of Congress Cataloging-in-Publication Data

Rineberg, Dave, 1965-
Play scratch golf : the amateur golfer's guide to playing perfect golf / Dave Rineberg.
    p. cm.
ISBN 0-88391-170-1 (pbk. : alk. paper)
1. Golf--Amateurs' manuals. I. Title.
GV965.R545 2008
796.352'3--dc22

                    2008026742

ISBN-13   978-0-88391-170-9
ISBN-10   0-88391-170-1

Play Scratch
GOLF

AN AMATEUR'S GUIDE TO PLAYING PERFECT GOLF

ACKNOWLEDGEMENTS

A special thanks to PGA professional Chris Holtrop for his enthusiasm to write this book with me and share his knowledge and tour playing experiences with you.

For the beautiful book cover and interior design a great thanks goes to my friend and graphic artist: Elena Solis

Thanks to Dave Rempel for his workouts in the gym and his caddying at all amateur events.

Thanks to professional model Brittany Wagner for her appearance in the book.

For Frederick Fell Publisher's enthusiastic reception and speedy response to getting this book to print.

AUTHOR'S NOTE

The formula for becoming a scratch golfer is a complicated one, simply because of the fact that there is more than one way to hit a golf ball. As a competitive amateur player myself, I know that my golf swing and approach to the game of golf has gone through numerous changes. From the moment I first picked up a club to hit balls alongside my father on the range until this very day, I too have been searching for ways to hit the golf ball longer, stick it tighter and roll it in from virtually everywhere on the green. Going from a high handicapper to a scratch golfer has certainly been a journey for me but a journey full of life that I wouldn't trade for anything in the world. With golf's hole-by-hole and shot-by shot highs and lows, I've learned a lot about who I am, what I fear and who I want to be. The dream of one day playing professional golf that we've all had as kids still resurfaces every time I hit a booming drive to within go distance on a par five hole, pure an iron to within gimmie range on a well-guarded green or roll in a downhill double-breaking putt from the greenside fringe.

The truth of course is that only a small percentage of golfers will ever succeed and indeed capture the dream of becoming a PGA Tour Professional. For the rest of us golfers though, that doesn't change our love of this game nor our willingness to go to the range and pound balls for hours on end, change to the latest golf equipment or take numerous golf lessons if it will indeed help in our pursuit of a lower handicap. Now I've been what they call a feel player for most of my golfing life using my athleticism and touch to get me around a golf course. But in playing this game as a feel player, I found out that there are really only two kinds of days you can have on the golf course: good days and bad days. And it was those bad days that were keeping me from becoming a scratch golfer. In order to become a scratch golfer, I had to become more consistent, which meant I needed to be able to repeat a good swing even if I wasn't feeling the swing that particular day. In other words, "I needed technical help." This book is a compilation of that help and the most successful tips that have helped me lower my handicap. But even if your goals are not as lofty as mine were and golf is merely an enjoyable walk to you, this book still has a lot to offer to make that walk even more enjoyable.

This book is a breakdown of: a modern swing & the must have shots, up-to-date physical fitness & mental toughness training methods, playing strategies and tactics to help you score, all with a little philosophy from the mind of a coach and feel player mixed throughout. To include all the information that is out there would be lengthy so I've teamed up with PGA golf professional Chris Holtrop who teaches in perfect detail what I believe to be the best of the best necessities and the fastest way for you to drop 1-5 strokes off your score if you are already a low handicapper and 10-20 strokes off your score if you are a high handicapper.

The lessons, tips and stories herein are written first for you, the serious competitive golfer, who by reading this book, is taking the all-important first step to improve, refine and problem solve every facet of your game. Because as you know in this individual sport, there is no help out there once you are on the course. It is all up to you and what's deep inside you as to just how good your golf swing and shot making skills will get and to just how low you will score. Secondly, it is written for all the weekend warriors out there who don't have time to practice that much during the week and need those quick fixes, reliable swing thoughts, and stroke cutting tips in order to continue to enjoy this great game to its fullest. I hope this book can help give those of you on both paths a recipe for golfing success!

INTRODUCTION
Golf: The Game of a Lifetime

What is it about this game that we love so much? At the same time, what is it that we hate so much? Why is it that golf brings out seemingly every emotion known to man? Golf is just a game, right? For some it's a hobby and a past time. Then there are those for whom it is a passion. Golf engulfs their being, swallows them up, and won't let go. How is it that this game that was invented so long ago has captured the interest of so many people in so many different ways?

Golf is played under our free will, by our own choice. For some golf is a weekend pastime, a breath of fresh air and a chance to get out of the house. For others every day of the week is their pleasure. However, for most, golf is yet another form of entertainment, recreation, or even relaxation.

Golfers will pay money, often-large amounts of money to purchase the necessary and sometimes un-necessary equipment to play the game. The golf enthusiast will pay big money to access tournaments with the best players in the world, with hopes of stealing a glimpse of what it is like to play the game effortlessly at the highest level. A golf nut will overpay to play in tournaments, or belong to the local country club with the reason being; the opportunity to play the game. A golf junkie will travel seemingly endless distances to find the greatest course ever built and nothing will get in their way.

A die-hard will gather with friends, family, and sometimes with complete strangers spending four-plus hours every chance they get just to play this game. What is this intense passion, this obsession, this un-explainable enthusiasm for golf? Where did it come from and how exactly did it start? What is it about this game that lures us in and traps us in its grasp? What gives a game such drawing power, such attention, such intrigue? Sports writers and talk show hosts have been after the solution to this answer for years. Many have tried to answer this question but really, there may be no complete answer. There may not be an answer that can be accepted and used by everyone.

Over the last ten years, the number of golfers worldwide has multiplied dramatically. In 1996, it was estimated that there were 3.6 million golfers in the United States alone. This number identified approximately 76% of golfers worldwide. Today, there are an estimated 76 million golfers worldwide. The United States makes up only 23% of these golfers just 11 years later. The global expansion of golf is overwhelming and the increases are on the borderline of being astounding.

I have been playing golf since I was 6 years old. I've spent a good portion of my life investing myself in the game of golf. I was riding my bike 4 miles from my home in Michigan to the driving range at The Grand Rapids Golf Club in Grand Rapids, Michigan to wash the range balls four days a week when my service to the golf industry officially began. Currently, I am the Head Golf Professional at a Country Club in Boca Raton, Florida. I have been a PGA member for nine years and counting. I have played countless rounds of golf. Some rounds have been for fun with my friends and family. I have played with the members of the private country clubs where I have worked, and I have played competitively with high school and college golf teams. I have been fortunate enough to play in numerous professional tournaments competing against some of the best players the game has ever seen. My time in golf has been wonderful to this point.

Through all of this, I have met some amazing people and I have been to many stunning places. I have developed great friendships and been very fortunate to have traveled the world over playing this game, sometimes for fun, other times to compete. I have seen some of the most beautiful places on earth as golf courses are often built on the best pieces of real estate in the world. It is as if a developer finds a perfect piece of land and realizes that a housing development or a high-rise condo complex wouldn't do the piece of property the justice. Instead, he builds a golf course. Golf courses have the most beautifully manicured landscape you will find. Lush exotic plants and flowers, gigantic old trees standing the test of time, and rolling hills that seems to have endless possibilities.

Some of the most memorable times in my life have come with two common denominators. The first, spending time with my father and the second, being on a golf course. A number of years ago he and I took a wonderful trip the Monterrey Peninsula in California. For those of you who have been to this area, you will know that the Monterrey Peninsula and its surrounding area offer some of the most breathtaking scenery in the world. We played one round at Poppy Hills the first day and then endured a day at Spyglass on a rainy, foggy, and cold day. It was that third and final day of our trip that I recall so vividly. It was a spectacular day at The Pebble Beach Golf Links. The day proved to be the most brilliant day, seventy-three degrees and sunny and no wind. Our experience that day included the opportunity to play with a good friend of mine from college, Dave Johnson who was working in the Monterrey Peninsula area at Rancho Canada Golf Club. After the round while in the famous and historic lodge at Pebble Beach enjoying a drink the bartender told us the natives were lucky to see a dozen days a year that were as perfect as that day. The golf wasn't great that day. I should clarify and say the quality of the golf wasn't great that day. The golf experience however; was the best of my life. Having the chance to spend six hours with my father, a good friend from college, and a complete stranger on that golf course and on a beautiful day like this one, was nothing short of perfect.

I talk about this story because it is one of the many stories involving golf that has left me with an answer to that longing question that life so often asks... WHY. The ability the game of golf has to compel you to look inside yourself is intriguing and addictive. When you are on a golf course, you see all of the different emotions inside yourself. You face thousands of obstacles and potential decisions each time you step on the golf course. Each time you play, you encounter these feelings and run into these roadblocks. You face doubts, you challenge fear, and you are given the chance to prove to yourself what you are made of. If you think you always succeed, you are severely mistaken. Anyone who has ever played golf knows that you are likely to fail much more frequently than you will succeed.

It is this quest for something greater than results that I believe is the reason golfers are so fascinated with the game. As human beings, we are often judged on the results we produce. In the business world, more revenue and less expense lead to the biggest bottom line, which is what business is predicated on. An artist is judged by the final painting that is displayed to be critiqued by those so-called experts. Basketball teams are seen as great only when they win. Children are judged at school based on the final grade that shows up on their report card. The world is filled with endless examples of being classified as success or failure based solely upon the finished product, the bottom line, and the end result.

The fundamental process of golf asks the player to pick a target, select a club, and hit the ball to the target. The fewer strokes it takes you to get the ball to the target, the better. The difference in golf is that there is no such thing as perfection. There is no end result. Sure, there is PAR, which the governing bodies of golf have created to satisfy our human desire of a result. The truth is that PAR is a number relating historical data that is proven one day, but could be disproved later that same day. PAR is actually based on numbers that an imaginary scratch golfer would shoot, but there is no realistic, acceptable bottom line. In other words, there is no right answer. No one can say what you should or shouldn't do. It is one hundred percent up to the individual playing the game to decide what status quo is.

Reality is that each individual golfer is playing the game against no one else but himself or herself. They have no one to blame for their errant shots but themselves, they have no one to credit for the good shots, except themselves and they have no one to answer to when the round is over except, themselves. We have this built-in curiosity to want to know why. Most often, we want to know why things happen to us. When the desired results are missing and we feel we have done the right thing and don't deserve the results, we instinctively want to know why.

Golf gives you the chance to answer the question, why. Why did I hit that ball left? Why did I miss that putt? Why did I get so upset when I sliced that ball? Why did I choose that club? There are so many times we can ask, why? The answer lies within you the golfer; you just have to be willing to look for it.

Golf is a game that forces you to look within yourself to find the answers. It forces you to learn to control your thoughts, manage your emotions and to accept responsibility. All the while, you need to be concentrating with full intensity in order to hit your best possible shot. Golf allows you to use the free will that has been given to you to be confident and positive. Golf is not always easy on you, but one thing is for sure, golf will give you the chance to answer that question, why?

At the end of the day, when it is all said and done the only person you can look to for the answer is yourself. It is how you deal with your answer that makes golf such a great game! — Chris Holtrop, PGA Professional.

9 HOLES

CHAPTER

1

The Fundamentals

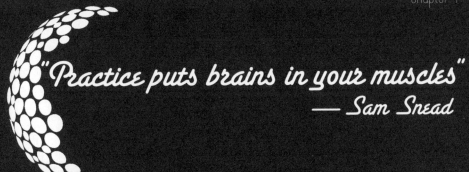

THE STARTING POINT

When I was in middle school, I was on the track team. I wasn't what you call blazing fast, but I could hold my own in most races. I certainly wasn't the fastest guy in the city, or the conference, and in most races on my own team. I ran track mostly to stay in shape for the other sports I played. Track was the one sport where my goal wasn't to win.

As with all other sports, there is a definite relationship with the mental side of running a race and the physical technique of running. My coach used to make us run a drill that has since served as a great mental analogy that has stuck with me into my golf career. I use this analogy often with new students as I am getting to know them and their golf games. More importantly, I use this story to let them know what I believe whole-heartedly as a teacher.

My coach would tell us to line up at the starting line and he was going to time us with a stopwatch once around the track. He would yell, "Go" and we would all shoot off as fast as we could. Rounding the first turn we would stay to the inside part of the lane and push our breath out of the stomach in order to circulate our air more efficiently. Our strides were long and our kick high and consistent. Maintaining our pace, controlling our breath, pumping the arms, keeping the head up and eyes forward, and pushing ourselves to the limit for the entire circle around the track was the only thought going through our head. The moment we crossed the finish line coach would stop the watch and look down at the time. Then he would read off the time and tell us to walk around for a few minutes. Then he would tell us to walk part way around the track to the next starting position to get ready to go again. Then he would explain that he was going to time us with the stopwatch from that different starting position. We would repeat this process from the four different starting positions on the track and that would be considered a set of training runs. Each time coach would call out our time it would be different.

The goal of the drill from a track standpoint was to split our times relative to the position on the track where we started, in other words if we started half way around the track, our time should be as close to half as what our initial time for a full lap. The significance of the analogy is the fact that each time I started from a different spot on the track, I would have a different time. No matter how consistent my stride, no matter how perfectly matched each kick, each breath, and every pump of the arms were, and no matter how hard I ran each time the results were always different.

In golf, this holds true more prominently than any sport I have ever seen. If you start your golf swing from a different position on every swing the likelihood of you repeating the motion part of your swing becomes quite unlikely. However; if you begin your golf swing using the same GRIP, the same STANCE, the same POSTURE, and with the same BALL POSITION and proper ALIGNMENT every time, you have the best chance to repeat the technique with timing and rhythm.

Many golfers begin a round of golf with optimistic confidence and high hopes for a great day on the links. They may begin with some good shots and even string together a few good scores to start the round. Inevitably, during the round every player is going to encounter adversity. This is the point where many players begin to feel uncomfortable, mostly because of the poor results they have just produced on previous shots. The first thing that an uncomfortable and unconfident golfer wants to do is to change something so they get back into some sort of comfort level. This commonly results in making a change before they even start the swing. For example, if a player keeps hitting the ball off to the right, the first thing many will do is to move their alignment to the left to compensate for the recently developed slice. If a player is hitting the ball thin or even topping the ball, they may bend over more to get the sensation of being closer to the ball. Often if a player is hooking the ball, they will move the right hand over on top of the club to give the feel of not being able to release the club as freely. Each of these are examples of how golfers manipulate their set up position, also known as the pre-swing fundamentals, in an effort to gain control over what is happening while the golf club is in motion.

While running around the track, I focused on maintaining my stride and kick much like I try to swing the golf club with the same feeling every time. Just like the analogy of my coach timing me back in middle school, if you don't start from the same place each time the likelihood of your results being the same are diminished greatly. When you change your starting position, no matter how good you have become at repeating the motion part of your swing, you are most likely not going to be able to produce the same results on a consistent basis.

The five fundamentals are the lifeblood of your golf swing. If the fundamentals are not where they need to be then you are going to struggle to ever improve your golf swing. Your consistency will suffer and your power will be non-existent. If you are still learning your golf swing, before you continue to your next step, you need to make sure that your fundamentals are the base of everything you are doing. Go through the five fundaments.

THE FIVE FUNDAMENTALS
1. The Grip
2. The Stance
3. Posture
4. Ball Position
5. Alignment

THE GRIP

The grip is the backbone of your entire golf swing. It has a relationship with every part of the golf swing including the rest of the set-up, the path the club travels, and the impact position. How it relates is quite complicated but without a good grip, you will have a very tough time building a good golf swing.

There are many choices when it comes to a good golf grip. Many good players have had many different grips. For younger or weaker players a strong grip is often recommended. This means that, for a right-handed golfer, the left hand will be well rotated to the right as it sits on the club.

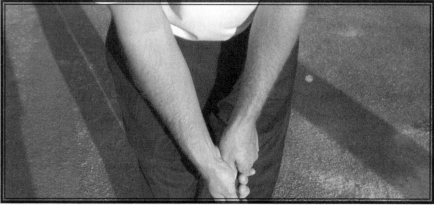

This is a strong grip. Notice the right hand rotated to the right side of the club

As you get better, bigger, or stronger you will often find it beneficial to weaken your grip towards a more neutral position. A neutral position means that the left hand will sit more on top of the club, but be sure that you can still see at least two knuckles on your left hand as you look down from your address position!

This is a neutral grip. The right hand sits on top of the club

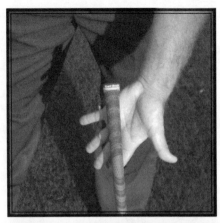

The left hand, for right-handed golfers, is the dominant hand as you hold the club. The handle of the club should run diagonally across the pads of your fingers. The handle will lay from the base of your forefinger and run across the pad just below the base of the pinkie finger.

The club should run along the pads of your left hand

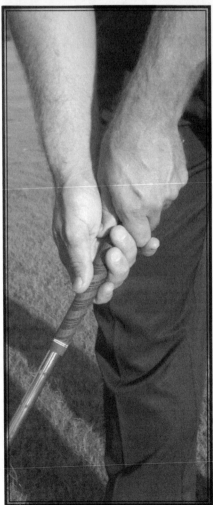

It is important to make sure the handle of the club doesn't get too close to the palm of the hand. Keeping the grip in your fingers helps to provide the best combination of feel and control. As you lower the club to the ground the left thumb will be slightly to the right of center, or at the one o'clock position on the handle. The 'V' that is formed between the thumb and the forefinger should be pointing up between the right ear and the right shoulder depending how strong or weak the grip.

The right hand works in conjunction with the left hand, and not coincidentally it sits on the club similar to the left hand. It is critical to get the handle of the club well into the fingers of the right hand. This will help insure the speed that the grip helps generate through the downswing. The handle should contact the right hand around the middle of the index finger and connect until near the base of the pinkie finger.

This is the conventional overlap grip in a neutral position. Notice how the handle of the club is controlled by the fingers only

THE 3 MOST COMMON GRIPS ARE:
1.The Interlock Grip
2.The Overlap Grip
3.The Ten-finger or Baseball Grip

These three grips are the most commonly used and taught by almost all golf instructors. There really isn't one that is right or one that is wrong. It is really the personal preference of each individual, however there may be some individual physical characteristics that may influence which are best for you.

1.The interlock grip is often referred to as the control grip.

The interlock grip

In the interlock grip the right pinkie finger is meshed between the forefinger and middle finger of the left hand. This gives the sensation that the hands can't separate during the swing and thus gives you the ultimate control in the golf swing. Two of the greatest players of all time use the interlocking grip: Jack Nicklaus and Tiger Woods. Players with large hands or longer fingers often gravitate to the interlock grip even though it is well know that Nicklaus had small hands.

The overlap grip

2.The overlap grip is where the pinkie finger of the right hand is placed in the notch between the forefinger and middle finger on the left hand.

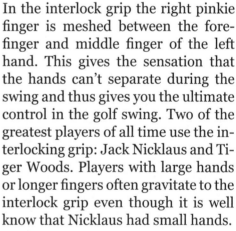

Although this grip still has a snug feeling, it gives a sense of more freedom throughout the swing. The majority of golfers and golf instructors prefer this version to the other two, most likely because of the versatility that the grip provides.

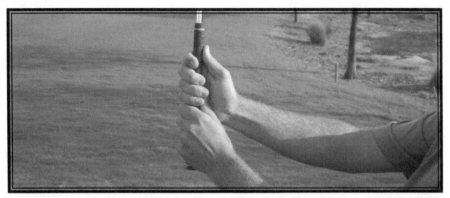

The ten-finger grip; also known as the baseball grip

Young golfers or golfers with small hands are often encouraged to use the ten-finger grip to accommodate the size of their hands. The ten finger grip is exactly what it says, all ten fingers touch the handle of the club while the thumb of the left hand sits just right of the center of the handle and fits into the lifeline crease on your right hand. Many junior players begin using the ten-finger grip and then transition to the overlap or interlock as they grow bigger and stronger.

When it is all said and done, the most important aspect of the grip is that it provides you with a sense of solid control and unity between the two hands. It is critical to everything else that you do in the golf swing to have your hands feel like they are working together. If your hands are working together they will be able to hold the club with a consistent pressure. A pressure that is light enough to allow your wrists and forearms to be tension free, but firm enough to maintain control over a driver traveling at 100 mph or more. The key to good grip pressure is that it stays the same throughout the swing. Many players have the tendency to start with good grip pressure at address and then proceed to squeeze harder and harder throughout the swing. This happens most often because of a flawed grip to begin with when players instinctively grab the club when it accelerates toward the ball. If you develop a solid grip it will allow you to concentrate on the other areas of the swing that will help promote more consistent ball striking.

TOP 5 GRIP DRILLS

1. HAVE A CLUB TO HOLD... Put a club next to your couch for when you are watching TV or in your office during down time so you can pick it up and re-grip the club as often as possible. It takes doing something 30 times a day for 60 straight days or 60 times a day for 30 straight days to create a habit.

2. HOLD THE CLUB WITH ONE FINGER... and try to pull it out of your hand. If you have the handle of the club correctly positioned along the pads of your fingers the tension created from the position will make it nearly impossible to tug the club out of your hand. When you perfect this position you will know that you have the handle in the right spot.

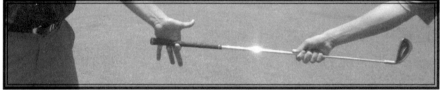

Hold the club with one finger to ensure proper placement in the hand

3. HINGE AND CHECK DRILL: From your address position lift the club straight out in front of you with your arms fully extended. Make sure your elbows stay straight throughout the drill. From that point cock your wrists so the club is pointing vertically up and down. The butt end of the club should be pointing straight down with the club head pointing up to the sky. At this point take the palms of both hands off the handle of the club. If you are still able to hold on to the club you will notice that it will be held by only your fingers. If you find yourself needing to adjust your hands and fingers before you let go, this will be a good indication that your hands are not properly positioned on the club to start with.

Hold the club in front of you, extend your arms, hinge the wrists, and take the palms off the handle to check if you are truly holding the club with your fingers

4. POINT THE V'S: While in your set up position, with the club head square on the ground your thumb and forefinger on each hand will create a "V" that will point up to your right shoulder (for right handed players) If you notice your V's pointing somewhere else other than your right shoulder, you may want to re-adjust your grip. Keep in mind that one "V" may be pointing in the right direction, and the other "V" in a different direction. If this happens, you will want to adjust the "V" that isn't pointing toward your shoulder. The hands need to work together while swinging the golf club and when the natural "V's" are pointing in opposite direction this indicates that your hands are opposing each other in the swing. When this happens it forces other areas of your body to manipulate the club in order to get to the desired impact position.

5. CORRECT PRESSURE: Take a long straw and place it between the club handle and the 'V' of the left hand. Take a few swings trying not to crush the straw or let it slip out.

Notice the two "V's" parallel and pointing toward the right shoulder

THE STANCE

The golf swing is a combination of multiple motions from all different areas of the body. There are many different parts moving different directions at different speeds. You need a solid stance in order to support all of these movements while swinging the club.

The stance is critical for both balance and power. It is important that you don't get your stance too wide and at the same time you don't want to be too narrow. A wide stance will give you plenty of balance and stability; however you will have a hard time generating much power in order to create club head speed. As a rule-of-thumb, the wider your stance, the less you will be able to rotate your hips and shoulders on both the backswing and downswing. Likewise, a narrow stance will give you more range-of-motion for a longer turn, but your balance and stability will suffer when you try to generate more and more speed.

Too narrow of a stance can cause balance issues   Too wide a stance will hinder necessary movement in the swing

The proper stance width will have a good blend to accommodate both a good turn with your shoulders and hips and at the same time give you enough support with your feet and legs to really go after the ball with some speed. The proper stance width will allow you to shift your weight from your right side to your left side while still maintaining the flex in your right knee on the backswing and allowing you to unload on your left knee (for right-handed players) during the downswing and follow thru while keeping your balance and stability throughout.

POSTURE
Athletic or Lazy?

Good posture is essential to all good athletes and very important with every sport that requires multiple movements from different parts of the body. With out good posture in athletics you will have less chance to control your muscle movements in order to perform the motion you are attempting.

Picture a baseball player playing the position of shortstop. When the pitcher delivers the ball to the hitter he is in an upright position with his eyes forward, his weight slightly forward. He is balanced and in position to move any direction required in order to make a play. For a baseball player to make a play on the ball it will potentially require him to move his legs in any direction towards the ball in motion. His eyes will need to remain on the ball at all times until the ball is in the glove, which will usually require the player to bend down and extend his arms to reach the ball. At this point the player will re-focus his eyes on the first baseman's glove, rotate his body, cock his arm and wrist, un-coil his body, turn his shoulders, and extend both arm and wrist to generate enough energy to help the ball travel the right distance in the right amount of time to beat the runner to the base.

In order for all of these steps to work together the baseball player must remain in a stable, consistent, athletic posture throughout the entire play. If at any point the shortstop were to lose balance, or slouch down, or let his head lower enough to lose sight of the ball his likelihood of getting the baseball to the first baseman in time diminishes greatly.

Let's consider a tennis player attempting to return a serve. She is balanced with a wide stance and proper bend at the hips and knees, her weight slightly forward in a ready position. Her eyes are forward and her head and torso is upright and centered over her base. She is on the balls of her feet and poised to move in any direction.

When her counterpart fires the serve in her direction she must pick up the direction, pace, and even spin of the ball and then react immediately to it. Her legs need to propel her in the direction of the quickly approaching ball so she can set her feet in the proper position to balance her body's motion of the tennis stroke. The player watches the ball as it approaches her racket and at the same time she rotates her body in a coiling motion and extends her arm away from the arriving ball. At the last moment the athlete then releases her body, her arm, shoulders and wrist while holding the angle of the racket in such a manner to hit the ball over the net in the perfect direction, angle, and with the right amount of spin.

The tennis player is reliant on her posture to remain strong, stable, and constant in order for her to hit the most consistent and powerful shots she possibly can.

Think finally of a quarterback in football. When he is preparing to take a snap from center he is bent down at the hips with his back straight, chin up, and eyes forward. His weight is balanced and he is ready to move in any direction.

All athletes rely on posture to support their movements

There are an infinite number of directions and options a quarterback could have at the time the football is snapped. He may have to dive forward under a pile and be prepared for a fight for the ball. He may have to turn either direction to hand the ball off or pitch it to a runner, or drop back in any certain fashion to throw the ball. Each motion this quarterback is asked to make require all parts of his body working together to produce the results required to play winning football. If he gets lazy with his posture, he will be less likely to get to that fumbled ball, or make that laser beam throw over the middle of the field when it comes time to perform his best.

Posture in golf is more important than all of the previously discussed sports and any others as well. Posture in the golf is the axis in which the golf swing turns around. When you have good posture that is fail-proof, your chance of hitting good quality golf shots increases dramatically.

Your posture should start you feeling athletic and strong. Golf requires movement from many different areas of the body. It is critical for you to be in an athletic-ready position so that you can quickly respond to the movements made in the microseconds of the golf swing. While you are responding to these movements it is essential that you stay balanced and under control.

Good Posture is maximized when the torso and the lower body are working together to react to the motions of the swing throughout it. The point where you torso and lower body meet is at the hips and pelvis. Proper posture begins here. The feeling you want to have is that of sticking your fanny away from the golf ball. This creates the proper bend between your upper and lower body. Your belt buckle should be pointing down towards the ball. This bending point acts as a support for your upper body to rotate around throughout your golf swing. Maintaining this angle in your hips is critical to the consistency in which you make contact with the ball.

Tilting the hips is where good, athletic posture begins

Once you learn the proper bend in the hips you can move down to the bend in your knees. The knees should have a relaxed, natural bend to them. Some taller players may find it necessary to bend more at the knees, while shorter players will feel more erect in the knees. Every player will be a little different in this area as we are all different physiological beings. It is important not to be too deeply bent in the knees and conversely we want to avoid the straight-legged golf swing. Once you find your proper knee bend it is very important to maintain that flex throughout much of the swing.

The picture to the right is a common look for many amateur players. This amount of bend makes it very difficult for the player to make a complete turn both on the backswing and downswing. The consequently shorter swing will cost them club speed and ultimately distance as well as accuracy. The inability to turn from this common problem causes the club head to point left and can cause pulls and slices.

The feeling of sitting down is not the best choice for golfers

If the knees are locked at address your sense of balance is lost along with the ability to maximize power because of the need to bend excessively at the waist just to reach the ball. The lower body is virtually taken out of the swing and the upper body performs the entire motion. The result is short shots that should be going much further.

Locking the knees hurts balance
through the swing

The picture to the right shows the proper bend in the knees. With a good bend, you are now ready to create the action required for good golf swings. You are balanced and have a sense of being light on your feet. You can now get your lower body working together with the upper body throughout the entire swing.

The proper bend in the knees helps you
stay comfortable and balanced

The angle of the torso is quite possibly the most important aspect of posture. Your flexibility and strength of your back, shoulder, and neck muscles will affect your ability to create this most-important angle. The best way to describe this angle is by drawing a picture. If you hold the head of one of your irons and rest the top end of the club-head on top of your head while the shaft runs all the way down your spinal column to the top of the tailbone. The key here is the shaft should be touching you in as many constant places along your back as possible. There should not be any noticeable large gaps between the club and your body. With the club along your back you should address the ball with the club hanging straight down from the shoulders and the body leaning forward slightly.

The angle of the torso should be straight
indicating good posture and the best
chance to hit great shots

This angle must stay consistent throughout the swing to insure solid contact at impact. The most aggravating piece of advice in golf is to "keep your head down." What this so called "advice" is really referring to is the angle of the torso. Since the head is connected to the torso via the neck it then follows the every move that the torso makes. For example if the torso were to change its angle to be more vertical during the swing, the players head would move "higher" at that point. Instead of thinking of burying your head in your chest next time someone tells you to keep your head down, think of maintaining the angle of your torso throughout the entire swing and chances are you will hit solid shots much more frequently.

The angle of the torso remains constant through the backswing

Your center-of-gravity is a term that golfers need to be familiar with. Center-of-gravity is where your body's ultimate balance point is located. The center-of-gravity (COG) is located at a spot somewhere in the mid-section of your torso. Often, I will describe your COG as the place just below the bottom of your shirt placket on your traditional style golf shirt. This COG is also your center of balance and timing. It is the point in which the motion of your body feels like it belongs, or doesn't belong. Dancers, figure skaters, gymnasts, tennis players and martial artists all are known for having tremendously keen sense and awareness of center-of-gravity. It's not a coincidence that these athletes have tremendous balance and body control. COG awareness is important to the ability to have consistent control over their swing.

To have the proper balance and weight disbursement in your set up position it will be important in your posture to have your COG moved slightly forward. Out past your toes is where I like to see it. An analogy I like to use is that I want you to feel like you are standing on the edge of a cliff and trying to peak over the edge to see what's down below. You aren't going to be so far bent over that you lose your balance, but you will be stable, and your COG will feel slightly forward over your toes.

Position your weight forward for the best results

It is also important to understand the relationship of your COG with the ball at the address position. When we talk about the motion part of the swing we will get into the importance of moving your COG behind the ball and keeping it behind the ball until impact. This will be one of the more detailed features we discuss. For the set up, it makes sense to me that we want the COG to be in a position to move in the proper direction when we start the swing.

The COG should be tilted slightly behind the ball at the address position. The tilt should be initiated just above the right hipbone (for right-handed players) and just below the bottom of the rib cage. The tilt should only be felt in the torso. There should be no shift of the lower body when moving your COG slightly to the right.

Proper tilt behind the ball

Center of gravity centered over the ball leaving no room for error

Torso tilted behind the ball with the hips moving too far forward can create lateral hip motion during the swing

This tilt helps to initiate the proper backswing and helps to encourage the COG to turn behind the ball as the swing begins. As you read through the instruction part of this book as it relates to the full swing you will discover this COG tilt to be critical to creating a swing that produces consistent results.

BALL POSITION
Where Does It Go?

One of the most frequent questions as it relates to ball position is, "where do I put the ball in my stance?" The answer is not quite as simple as it seems it should be. Many great players have had various opinions on this question, and all have proven success with what they believe. Years ago players would always say that all shots should be played off the left heel, or forward in the stance. This ball position will naturally help the player turn behind the ball regardless of the motion they make while taking the club away from the ball. This concept is OK as long as you understand how it will affect your shots with every club.

Ball positioned off the left heel for all shots is not as common these days

Many high handicap amateur players have the idea that ball position should be off your back foot or back in your stance. They claim that this helps them feel that they can consistently hit down on the ball and therefore make good solid contact more often. What the amateur doesn't realize with this theory is that by putting the ball back in your stance will encourage some very bad habits that will send you into a tailspin of poor swinging. I have seen good players who are decent ball-strikers turn into some of the most inconsistent players due to this thinking. Many players will often play their longer clubs too far back in their stance, thus creating a downward chopping motion that forces the player to trap the ball against the ground with the clubface. This is done because many times the player doesn't feel like he/she can reach all the way to the ball with the longer clubs if the ball is placed towards the front of the stance. The problem this creates though is that you can't turn behind the ball fully on the backswing, which will result in pop-ups, pulls, slices, and chunks. Notice there is no consistency in your misses at this point!

Ball position too far back in the stance creates a trapping feeling that can get the ball moving anywhere and everywhere

THE BEST THOUGHT ON BALL POSITION

The best thought on ball position is that ball position actually changes depending on the length of the club that you are using. With your wedges and your shorter irons, the bottom of your swing will come sooner than with your longer irons therefore you need to position the ball close to the middle of your stance. This will encourage a downward blow on the ball, which will allow you to put some spin on the ball to help control both the flight and the spin when the ball lands. As you move up to your middle irons, the ball position will move forward slightly. The bottom of the swing actually moves back a little as the irons get longer, but the need to hit down on them becomes less important. It is more important to control the trajectory of your mid irons to reduce the amount of spin you create by hitting down too steep on the ball. By moving the ball a couple of inches forward of center it allows you to hit the ball when the club head is just beginning its upswing. This will keep the friction that is caused from the club hitting the ground, grass, and ball to a minimum making it easier to control the trajectory and spin.

The long irons, hybrid clubs, and fairway woods will move even further forward in the stance for much of the same reason. In addition to reducing spin and controlling trajectory, moving the ball further forward with these clubs will allow more time for the body to react to the turn behind the ball. As we will discuss later in more detail, turning behind the ball is essential to consistent golf shots. The longer the clubs get, the more difficult it is for you to control the motion of the swing especially at the critical transition point where the club stops going back and then starts going forward. By moving the ball forward in the stance, off the left heel if you are right handed, this allows for you to sense a better turn and have more time to re-turn back to the ball.

For all the same reasons, the ball position with the driver should be further forward in your stance than any other club. Position the ball off your left instep. Most important with the driver is the ability and sensation that you have of turning behind the ball. With the driver it also allows you to extend your arms into the ball thus creating the maximum club head speed at impact.

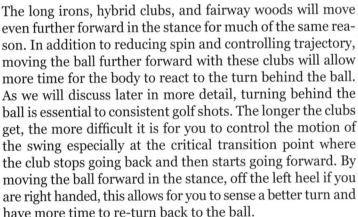

Pic 1—Short irons- ball position in the middlew
Pic 2—Mid irons – ball position between middle and left heel
Pic 3—Hybrids/Long irons/ Fairway Woods just short of the left heel
Pic 4—Driver placed off the left heel

Improper ball position is one of the most damaging aspects of a golf swing. At the same time, correct ball position will help encourage the right moves during the swing. It is very important to place the ball in the correct position in relation to which club you are hitting and the good stance that you have developed.

Standing the correct distance from the ball is related to both ball position and posture. Standing the proper distance from the ball is significant to making good, consistent swings. Regardless of the club you are using, your hands should always be the same distance from your body. Different clubs will require you to place the ball farther away from your body; there should never be the sensation that you are reaching for the ball. Conversely you should never feel crowded or restricted when addressing the ball. The ball will be closer to you with the shorter clubs, but your hands will remain the same distance from your body. With the driver, fairway metals, and long irons the ball will be further from you, but you must resist the temptation to reach.

Pic 5—Too close to the ball
Pic 6—Too far from the ball
Pic 7—THE PERFECT distance from the ball

ALIGNMENT
How To Aim

Aiming is all about perception but since none of us perceive anything exactly the same way, this makes the concept of aim very difficult to explain. Alignment is directly related to your ball position. If one of them is wrong then the other is most likely wrong as well.

Next time you go to a PGA Tour, LPGA Tour, Champions Tour, or Nationwide Tour event take a few minutes to go to the driving range and observe the players practicing. There is one thing that I can guarantee you will see; players will all have something or someone to help them with their alignment on every full swing they take. I promise that each player will have one of their other 13 clubs lying on the ground pointing at their target, or maybe they will use their umbrella for the straight-edge, and quite possibly some of them may have invested in a little wood stick that acts as their guide while going through their routine. If you don't happen to see something on the ground, you will then most likely see either the caddy or better yet their own personal coach standing on the target line of their choice poised to let them know when they get one or all of their different alignment spots out of whack. The point is that every one of the best players in the world thinks it is very important to pay attention to alignment on every shot. If alignment is this important to the best players in the world then it must be in your top five as well.

Use a club to monitor your alignment

To get aligned, start by standing behind the ball and picking something near and far. When you stand directly behind the ball it helps to give you the perception of the exact line you intend to take to your target. (It also allows you the chance to actually pick a target...see chapter 13 for more on targets!) From behind the ball find a target in the distance on the line you want your ball to travel. Trace that line all the way back to the ball, but just before you get to the ball pick something out two or three feet in front of the ball that is on the target line. This will give you something close to the ball that will help you set up on target.

Find an intermediate target to help ensure perfect line up with the clubface

Next, think of a train-track. Your feet, your hips, and your shoulders represent the inside track. If you were to lay a club down across your toes, that club should be parallel to the inside track. If you were to lay a club across your hips and down your shoulder line, those too should be parallel to the inside track. When one of the parts are out of parallel with the rest this will create the feeling of parts opposing each other. This is one of the fastest ways to mess up the timing of a good golf swing.

Alignment should be parallel

The outside track starts at the ball and makes a straight line to the final target. Since the club head is making contact with the ball, you clearly want the head of the club to begin square to the target line, or in this case the outside track.

Lines indicate Perfect set up to target

It is the separation created from the length of the club and the athletic posture we have already discussed that causes the need for the train-track imagery method of alignment. All parts can't be pointing at the same exact point or else the perception will be confused and the body's timing will be out of sync.

One of the most common mistakes is to forget to take time to look at the target. Use your eyes to get yourself into a comfortable position. Many players get so involved in the movements and positions of the hands, legs, shoulders, and head that they simply ignore the fact that one glance could tell them that they are aimed nowhere near where they think they are. Perception, as it relates to alignment in the golf swing, is about training your eyes. Your eyes need to tell you whether or not you are properly aligned to the target of your choice. If you forget to use your eyes to check what you think you are doing, you will most definitely develop some very bad habits that can hinder your progress with your golf swing for a very long time.

Swivel the head to see your target line

CHAPTER SUMMARY
ESSENTIALS FOR PLAYING SCRATCH GOLF
THE FUNDAMENTALS

➤The Grip has a relationship with every part of the golf swing

➤As you and your game mature it is best to graduate towards a more neutral grip in an effort to keep unnecessary spin off the golf ball.

➤The Grip should always be in your fingers for full swings, not in the palm of your hand.

➤The "V's" formed by your thumb and index fingers on both hands should point in a parallel direction, for right handed golfers this will be somewhere near your right shoulder.

➤The stance is critical for both balance and power. The proper width stance will have a good blend to accommodate your hips and shoulders turn and give enough support to your legs and feet throughout the swing.

➤Good posture is essential for all sports but especially in sports, like golf, that require multiple moving parts from different areas of the body.

➤Golf is an athletic sport. It is very difficult to repeat the athletic motions required in the golf swing when attempting to perform from an un-athletic position.

➤Good posture is maximized when the torso and lower body are working together to react to the motions of the swing. Good posture starts in the hips with a feeling of sticking your fanny out and balancing your weight forward like peaking over the edge of a cliff.

➤Tilt your (COG) center of gravity slightly behind the ball at the address position. This encourages you to turn behind the ball and creates the opportunity to have a full, consistent weight shift.

➤Ball position changes from club to club depending on the length of the club being hit. Ball position never gets behind center and never further forward than off your left heel.

➤Your hands should always hang the same distance from your body regardless of what club you are hitting.

➤Alignment is about perception and everyone's perception is different. The best way to check alignment is to have someone watch you.

➤Always put alignment tools down to help train your perception. Use a club, umbrella, or anything long and straight.

➤Start behind the ball before every shot to see the line.

JUNIOR GOLFERS ESSENTIALS

➤It is important to learn the fundamentals but the exact positions are not as critical until you gain strength in your swing.

➤Juniors who start with a ten-finger grip should first move into a strong regular grip and then graduate into a neutral grip as you get bigger and stronger.

➤The Grip is most critical element to get right as you get older. Posture, stance, alignment and ball position are important as well but if you can first learn how to hold the club properly this will accelerate everything else you do in golf.

➤Learn a routine that takes you through a checklist of the fundamentals. This routine will stay with you for your entire golfing life.

TOURNAMENT PLAYERS ESSENTIALS

➤If you want to play competitive golf your fundamentals better not be a question mark. This is the area where you must find the perfect, repeatable set up that is comfortable and right for you as an individual.

➤Alignment and ball position are the two most likely sources for trouble in your golf swing. Routinely check them, every day if you can.

➤At least three times a year you should get together with your teacher or coach and spend some time reviewing your fundamentals. You can never spend enough time on them.

THE FUNDAMENTALS — The Great Equalizer

➤The fundamentals don't change from men to women or from junior to senior. Some of the specifics for the different ages or genders may differ but the principles stay the same.

➤Different individuals may physically be able to reach different fundamental spots for golf, but the athletic offering for all players is the same. Great fundamentals will help every player be that much better. Fundamentals do not discriminate.

CHAPTER

2

PUTTING

"Happiness is a long walk with a putter"
— Greg Norman

My old golf coach used to preach, "If you can't roll it, you ain't gonna score it. If you can't chip it to somewhere that you can roll it in from, you ain't gonna score it." Then he would finish his sermon by saying, "if you can't get it to somewhere that you can chip it or roll it in from, then you probably ought not be here."

During most rounds of golf you will have somewhere between one-quarter and one-third of all your shots taken with your putter. That means for every driver you hit, you will hit almost 2 1/2 putts. That's a lot! Think of your putter as your scoring club. Three average shots on a par-4 hole can still become par if you are good putter of the ball. Becoming a good putter of the ball though, is a process. A process that starts first in your head.

Putting is first and foremost about attitude. You have to believe you are a great putter in order to be a great putter. You have to cherish the opportunity to make a four-foot putt for the win. When you look at a putt, no matter how difficult, you have to see it going into the hole. You must believe that you are a great putter every time you play a round and to do that, you have to be willing to go out and put in the work to becoming a great putter. Wanting and willing are two different attitudes and no matter how much you want to become a great putter without the willingness to achieve you will never get there. There are a lot of great ball strikers on the mini-tours who are missing that willing to be great attitude. When you are playing a round and arrive at the green, get the attitude that this is where the game begins, this is where the fun begins. If you have that kind of attitude and that feeling of relief that now you finally get to putt, then you will have begun to have the right attitude of a great putter.

Having a positive attitude about your putting will help to breed confidence in you when on the greens. When you step over a putt you must feel that you can always make it. After sinking putt after putt, the cup will begin to look the size of a bucket and you will be able to consistently make a smooth, free putting stroke. It sounds easy to just change your thinking but what if you've tried telling yourself that you're a good putter and still you are not making any putts?

Every person alive has the God-given ability to make his or her own choices. When you look at a putt you have the choice to believe you are going to make it, or believe you are going to miss it. Notice I didn't say that you believe that you are capable of making the putt, I said you believe that you ARE GOING to make the putt. If you stand over a putt guessing, hoping, even praying that you make the putt than you are most likely not in the proper frame of mind. You aren't using the freedom to make your own choices to better your golf game. You are letting fear and negative thoughts choose for you. You have the choice to think whatever you want to think when you walk up to the green and get ready to putt so why not think positive. If you can make the commitment to approach every putt with a positive attitude, think that you are relieved to finally get to putt, and have thoughts of nothing but draining the putt before you, then you will become a better putter almost instantaneously.

One of the most impressive aspects of junior golf is the lack of fear that kids have when they are learning the game. Especially on the putting green, kids seem to have a sense of immortality. Have you ever noticed that when you give a kid a putter, a ball, and a four-foot putt and tell them to make it, they have no sense and certainly no care of what the meaning of that putt is. Whether they make the putt or miss it, it doesn't really matter to them. You can give them the same putt over and over again and kids just don't care if they make it or miss it. What a great attitude to have towards putting.

Up to one-third of your shots during a round of golf are made with your putter. The best putters realize the centrality of putting, yet they don't get too concerned about any one given putt. They treat each putt the same. You only have two possible results when you putt: you make it, or you miss it. Good putters have eliminated thoughts like, " I've got to make this putt," or "I really should make this putt. Regardless of the length or difficulty of the putt they treat every one of them the same.

Good putters realize that whether they make the putt or miss the putt, the world is not coming to an end because of it. They keep their heads up, they stay in the present, and they believe that they are going to make every putt.

THE PUTTING FUNDAMENTALS

There are certainly fundamentals to the putting stroke that are important if you truly expect to make a high percentage of putts. The fundamentals of putting much like the full swing, begins with the grip.

The Putting Grip

The putting grip is similar to the full swing grip in that there is not one right grip for any individual. There have been many great players who have had tremendous success with what is referred to as the conventional grip. You will no doubt however; be able to turn on the TV this weekend and see a wide variety of putting grips from many of the best players in the world. Grip styles such as the claw, cross-handed, split-handed, left hand low, and I could go on and on but you get the point. The question is then what is the correct grip for you?

The most important thing in putting, whether you are referring to the grip, the posture, the stance, the ball position or alignment is to be comfortable. You must feel good over the ball. On your longest putt the hands might move a total of 18 inches in either direction. Your arms move about half of that, and your shoulders even less. Your body will move hardly at all, and your head should stay perfectly still. So, your main priority when gripping the putter needs to be establishing the feeling of comfort, sensitivity, and relaxation.

The handle of the putter is going to run much closer to the palm of the hand than in the regular grip. In the full-swing grip the handle needs to stay in the fingers so there is a sense of control, yet flexibility so you can properly and freely release the golf club at the impact position but with the putter you don't need that much release action since the club is moving at much slower speeds. Where the handle sits in the palm of the hand can vary from player to player. I suggest letting the handle start at the fat part of the left hand closer to the fingers than to the wrist.

The putter handle runs in the palm of your hand

The back of the left hand should be facing the target in a square or what is known as a weak position. This will help to keep the hands from rotating during the stroke. The back of the right hand should be parallel to the back of the left hand. This will start the hands square to the target and working together throughout the stroke. Having both hands square in relation to the target will make it easier to keep the face of the putter square throughout the impact zone.

The palm of the right hand should fit over the left thumb comfortably. The left thumb should run parallel with the right thumb, which will be extending down the putter handle at twelve o'clock. The thumbs are as important to your feel in putting as the rest of the fingers and will provide the most feedback. Be careful not to extend either thumb too far down the shaft. This can cause tightening of your hands and wrists, which will keep your hands from working freely together.

The conventional grip was the pioneer of all grip styles therefore most of the other grip styles share many of the fundamentals of the conventional grip. Where the conventional grip separates itself from the pack is with the reverse-overlap grip. This is where the left forefinger lays across the top of the fingers of the right hand. This placement of the left forefinger provides a sense of agreement for the hands however it doesn't lock the hands together in any way. The other positive feature of the reverse-overlap grip is that it doesn't allow either hand to feel more dominant during the stroke.

Reverse overlap grip

Grip Pressure

Grip pressure is often overlooked when you think about the fundamentals of the putting stroke but it is critical to developing the feel it takes to make a lot of putts. The tendency for most players is to squeeze the putter too tight. I call it white-knuckle putting. In South Florida where I live, driving in traffic can be a tense and stressful time. When you are moving in stop-and-go traffic in the midst of semi-trucks, speeding cars, and torrential rain showers drivers have the tendency to grab the steering wheel with great intensity thus becoming white-knuckle drivers. While driving this may be a sense of security and control, while putting a four-footer this is the recipe for a miss. Intensity needs to be in your focus on the target, not in your hands. Next time you are on the putting green try holding the putter so lightly that you almost feel like you may drop it. You will find that you have a greater sense and feel of the putter head and the overall pace of the stroke. On a scale of 1 to 10, ten being the tightest, I would say the ideal grip pressure is a 4. This may vary from player to player but not by much.

Putting Stance

The putting stance like the rest of the putting stroke is an individual decision depending on comfort and feel. There is little movement in your torso and legs during the stroke that the width of your stance doesn't affect the motion of the putter. The width of the stance is more-or-less a matter of comfort to the player. Many players feel that a wider stance will give them a feel of stability and may help keep the body still throughout the stroke. Often in windy conditions players will widen their stance to help keep them more stable and with a feeling of being anchored to the ground. Some players feel that a narrow stance will allow them to stand taller over the ball and give them a better view of the line they are putting on.

Putting Posture

When talking about the posture in putting it is essential to focus on the placement of your eyes in relation to the ball and your target line. Posture starts in the hips similar to the set-up for the full swing. The hips should push your rear-end away from the ball thus creating the angle for your torso to lean towards the ball. Your torso and head should lean far enough over so that your eyes are placed directly over the ball and your target line. Your knees should be flexed comfortably. Too much knee flex will cause a strain in your back and force you to feel un-balanced. Not enough flex in your knees will cause you to lose balance and feel unstable over the ball. This will also make it difficult to get your eyes over the ball.

Not enough knee flex   Too much knee flex   THE PERFECT amount of knee flex

Getting your eyes over the ball is a great indication that your posture is good, you are the correct distance from the ball, and that you have the best opportunity to see the line that you are trying to putt along. Having your eyes placed directly over the ball is important for perception. If you believe you are lined up straight at the hole but looking at it from a position too far inside your target line, or too far outside your target line you will be giving yourself a false perception of what you are looking at. If you begin doing this on a regular basis you will start to train your perception to be incorrect. You will be telling yourself you are lined up straight when in reality you are lined up to the right or to the left. When you start missing putts consistently to one side or another you will naturally begin to alter your stroke to compensate. This is where many players mess up the potential to be better than they are.

MISSING PUTTS LEFT

If you are missing a lot of putts to the left the first thing you want to check is if you are standing too close to the ball, bending too much at the knees or waist, or somehow getting your eyes hanging out beyond the ball. Having your eyes beyond the ball causes you to perceive straight as being left.

Eyes too far over the ball can cause misses to the left

MISSING PUTTS RIGHT

If you are missing putts to the right you should check to see if you are standing too far from the ball, standing up too tall, or standing with little or no flex in your knees. These are all indications of seeing the line from too far inside the ball creating the perception that you need to swing the putter down a line that forces the putt to the right of your intended target.

Eyes too far inside the ball

Eyes right over the ball is universal for all good putters

What is truly important is that you have your eyes directly over the line in which you intend to hit the ball. Keep in mind that the line extends behind the ball as well as from the ball to the hole. It is acceptable for the head and eyes to set slightly to the right of the ball at the address position. (a right-handed player). It is difficult not to do this if you position the ball forward of center in your stance. It is very important that you keep your eye-line parallel to your target line while you are going thru your set-up and routine. As you check your target and glance back and forth from your target to the ball you will be continuously turning your head as if it is on a swivel. Be careful that this swiveling of the head doesn't turn into a lifting motion that can cause a dramatic change in eye placement in relation to your target line.

Swivel your head to see your target, don't stand up

You need a way to check to be sure that your eyes are not misplaced over the ball as you prepare to make your stroke. If you wear a cap or visor, a great way to check your eye alignment is to relate the position of the bill of the hat to the perception you have while looking directly over the line of the putt. Getting your eyes aligned over the ball may be the most important mechanical detail in the putting process.

Putting Ball Position

Ball position in putting is just as you would suspect, it's up to you the player to decide where the ball is placed based on comfort and feel. Typically you don't want your eyes to be ahead of the ball while looking down at it at the address position this can cause a downward hit on the ball that can cause backspin and make it difficult to judge distance. Most players put the ball in the middle of the stance or even slightly forward. The thought is that you want to make contact with the ball slightly past the bottom of the pendulum swing of the putting stroke. The further forward you place the ball in your stance the more you will contact the ball on the upswing of the stroke. Some players and teachers feel this is important in order to get the ball rolling sooner.

The ball slightly forward in your stance will help get the ball rolling quicker

Studies have been done and millions of dollars spent by many of the top putter manufacturers in the world to discover what it is that causes putts to go in the hole on a more consistent and frequent basis. One of the truths that have been proven because of these studies is that the golf ball, regardless of the type of grass surface you are putting on, sits in some varying degree of depression. Therefore the golf ball's natural tendency once struck will be to hop out of the depression. By increasing the loft of the putter, manufacturers say, the ball will hop less when struck because more loft is on the putter-face at impact. Also discovered is that by changing the length of the putter you can change the posture of the player so that they can more comfortably get their eyes over the ball in order to see the line of the putt better. The club manufacturers have hired intelligent people who know the physics of golf and the physiological motions that golfers make in an effort to develop clubs to sell to the mass number of golfers at all levels.

What can't be measured by any machine or determined from any study is the amount of heart a player has within. When it comes to putting, as stated earlier in this chapter, a positive attitude and belief in one's self can overcome any shortcomings you may have in your putting stroke. In order to have such an attitude and belief, you have to have heart. The world is full of people who will tell you that you can't do something or that you'll fail. It takes a person with inner courage, strength and heart to go out there and prove them all wrong. Be that person!

Routine, Routine, Routine

A great putting stroke requires good tempo, and a repeating, steady motion. One of the ways to accomplish a great stroke is to do everything with a good tempo, and with a repetitive, steady motion. The way to accomplish this is through a routine. I am referring to the pre-stroke routine or everything that you do before you start the putter in motion. Let's examine what a routine is and how it relates to your putting stroke.

The Webster's Dictionary definition of the word routine says, "routine, is a habitual or mechanical performance of an established procedure." To help you understand the definition further, take a look at the definition of the word procedure as well. Procedure is, "a series of steps followed in a regular, definite order." How does this relate to your putting routine? What needs to be agreed upon is the necessity for you to develop a routine that you will perform before every shot. According to the definition of routine what you do before every putt should be something habitual.

So what does it takes to create a habit? Studies show that it takes human beings performing an act 30 times a day for 60 straight days, or 60 times a day for 30 straight days in order to create a habit. So in order for you to create a habit of your pre-shot routine with your putter, you must consciously practice that routine for a long time.

The abbreviated definition of routine says, that you are creating a habit of a procedure, in this case the habit is of your pre-shot putting routine. The procedure or series of steps of your pr-shot putting routine, must be something that you have organized in your own head to an exact order. You then must teach yourself to follow these steps without conscious effort until you ultimately learn to trust your ability to repeat the routine without ever having to think about it. In other words, your pre-shot putting routine needs to become second nature. It needs to be something that you can rely on when you absolutely need to make a putt and it must be something that you don't have to search your mind to find.

Routines, like many parts of golf, are up to the individual. They can have many variations and steps to them. The key to any good routine, as you will be reminded constantly in the coming pages, is to execute it exactly the same every time. There are a few things you must decide when developing your putting routine, the first being, what is going to be your starting point or your trigger. The trigger is that point in time when your mind decides that the putt you are facing becomes the most important thing in your life and nothing else matters. Without an exact trigger, you can mess up the timing and the trust of your entire routine before it even begins. The trigger point is the beginning of your physical and mental routine, which we will discuss in further detail later. To illustrate this better, here is my personal putting routine.

MY PUTTING ROUTINE

When I approach a green and prepare myself to putt this is my routine. I start behind the ball with a quick glance at the line to see if I can get a feel for what path the putt will roll on. This however is NOT the beginning of my routine. When reading the putt (which we will talk about in more depth in the coming pages) I don't always do the same thing. I allow my feel for the putt to determine when I am ready to begin my routine. Sometimes I can look at the line from behind the ball and have a feeling that I know exactly what the ball is going to do so I go with my first instinct and begin my routine. Other times I am not sure so I will go to the opposite side of the hole to look at the line of the putt from that direction. Once I have determined what direction and how much the putt may or may not break I am ready to begin my pre-putt routine.

My trigger point is when I am holding the putter handle in my left hand and I lift the putter to waist height and rub the face of the putter with my right thumb. I decided on this trigger point a long time ago and became convinced that when I rubbed the putter face with my thumb that I was heating up the face so it would be hot and make a lot of putts. At the same time that my physical trigger point was happening, I was mentally starting to visualize my ball rolling into the hole at the exact point that I wanted it to enter. I always start my trigger from behind the ball.

Next, I take exactly four steps to get to the ball. My first step is always a long step and from that point I can shorten them if I need to in order to get the right spacing to get to the ball. The entire time I am approaching the ball I am focused on the hole allowing my eyes to translate the distance to the hole into my body so I can feel the exact distance I need to hit the putt. When I get to the ball I look down at it and keep myself far enough away from it, and then turn my eyes back to the hole. I take a slow, smooth practice swing that emulates the stroke I am about to make. During the practice stroke I am again gazing at the hole and focusing on a particular spot on the hole I want to see the ball enter. I briefly look back at the ball to get set up. I pay close attention to ball position, posture, grip, and stance. I lean my weight towards the target and take a deep breath as I look back towards the hole. Its almost time to go, but I am still thinking only about the part of the hole where the ball is going to go in. I take one last glance at the hole and as my eyes return to the ball I say to myself, "I'm going to make this!" and like clockwork I start the putter in motion.

The second most important thing about your putting routine is that you approach the ball 100% decisive about where you are going to hit it. If you aren't convinced and committed to what path the ball is going to take to the bottom of the cup, then your chances of making that putt have diminished greatly. It's better to be decisive about the line than right.

The third and final important part of a good putting routine is what happens just before you start the putter in motion. There needs to be a final glance at your target and the stroke needs to begin soon after that. If you stand over the ball too long then the likelihood of negative thoughts creeping in your head increases dramatically. In my routine I take one last look at the hole, bring my eyes back to the ball and the second my eyes are on the ball I consciously say the words, "I'm going to make this" and then I start the putter in motion.

A GOOD PUTTING ROUTINE HAS 3 THINGS:
1) A trigger point (both physical & mental).
2) A decisive approach.
3) A final look at the target.

One final word on putting routines, don't over do it! Some golfers have gotten the impression by watching professionals on TV that by taking more time to hit a putt or shot that they are going to have more success in the execution of that shot. That is completely false! All it does is slow down the pace and rhythm of play you're involved in, which then slows up the entire course. Nobody likes playing behind someone who double plumb bobs three-foot putts, takes multiple practice swings before each shot or backs off and then restarts after addressing the ball. In tournament play they monitor closely the pace of play and after a warning is given you are then penalized strokes for slow play. I believe if golf courses allowed the group behind to penalize the group ahead for unnecessary slow play, it would do away with the 4 1/2 and 5-hour rounds. Although, it might cause a few more fights and club throwing incidences on the course.

After playing one of the slowest rounds of my life behind a man in a bright yellow shirt in South Florida, I stopped into the 19th hole to get a sandwich and a drink for the ride home. While filling my soda at the sidebar, I noticed sitting at a nearby table, was the man in the bright yellow shirt. The same man who had slowed down the entire course to the point that on each hole there was a group behind the tee box waiting, a group on the tee waiting, a group in the fairway waiting all while he was on the green going through his ridiculously long putting routine. As more and more golfers came into the 19th-hole, all grumbling about how slow it was on the course, I over heard the man in the bright yellow shirt comment joyfully to his foursome, "What a wonderful day it was out there today. We didn't have to wait to hit on a single shot." My anger towards him quickly changed to laughter as I realized; the man in the bright yellow shirt, just didn't have a clue as to what he had done.

So remember, keep your routines simple. After all, the most important element of all routines isn't the length of the routine but that you can repeat it without fail, every time, no matter what!

Start your putting routine behind the ball

Take a practice stroke or two just like your intended stroke

Take one last look at the hole

Start your stroke in perfect rhythm

THE PERFECT STROKE

Mirror the Backswing and Follow Through

There are two common denominators in players who are labeled, good putters. The first is that they get their eyes directly over the target line when they set up to the putt and the second is that they always swing the putter head back-and-through, the same distance with the same pace.

Many aspects of putting allow you to be creative and feel the way you are most comfortable. After all, comfort is critical in putting. The idea of the putter blade going back and through with the same distance and at the same pace may be a bit un-comfortable to some but when you see someone with a silky smooth putting stroke the reason it looks so good is because the putter is taken back at a slow, even pace and then returned at the same pace. If you can learn to stroke each putt with a deliberate sense of tempo and rhythm from start to finish it will be much easier for you to keep the putter blade on-line and square. The idea is for you to avoid any sudden jerky movements through the stroke. When the putter makes a sudden movement it will most likely force the putter blade off line and cause a miss either to the right or left.

Although both arms are responsible for swinging the putter, it is much easier to let one of the arms be the dominant side. The most obvious would be to let your natural dominant hand act as the strong hand in your putting stroke yet some golfers find their opposite hand to have a better feel while making the putting stroke. Once you have decided which hand is going to act as your dominant hand, you must then in-fuse an acute sense of pace in that hand. By doing this you will allow yourself to trust that hand in your distance putting and it won't play the major role in your putting stroke. One of the best ways to do this is to practice putting with only your dominant hand.

While practicing with just the one hand you need to be cautious of two things: First, don't hold the putter too tight. There needs to be a certain amount of give or hinge in the wrist on the backswing to allow the put-ter to move freely. Keep in mind however, on the follow-through the wrist doesn't hinge any further than from where it started. You want the wrists to both stay quite and firm through impact. The putter will naturally feel heavier with only one hand holding it but by maintaining a light grip pressure you will develop a great sense of feel throughout the stroke. Secondly, be sure that you are concentrating on taking the putter back and through the same distance as well as at the same pace. The tendency will be to want to incorporate other body parts in order to help swing the weight of the club but keep the big muscles out of it and only use the arms and shoulders just as you would if you were u ing both hands.

Take the putter back and through the same distance

Tees in the ground show a Perfect, same distance finish

READING GREENS

One of the most difficult parts of putting for the amateur player is the science and art of reading greens. Yes, reading greens is an art. Because there are many factors that influence the green that you can't see, you must rely on your own creativity, guesswork, personal touch, experience and feel in your evaluation. On the other hand, there is certainly a definite amount of tangible, explainable science that you can see that you must factor in as well when reading a green. So it is safe to say that reading greens is a mixture of art and science or what you can see and what you can't see. To help understand what it is you should be looking for when reading greens, here are some of the tangible factors you need to consider.

Weather

One of the most affecting influences on putts is weather condition. The sun, rain and wind will all effect just how your ball will roll and the speed it will travel. A wind blowing more than 10 mph will cause your putt to lose speed, tail off line, or run further than expected. A light rain or dew on the greens in the morning will slow the pace of the putt. The grass on the greens is different heights at different times throughout the day.

The heights which greens are cut encourage rapid growth, which happens throughout the day. If you are playing in the afternoon the greens will be slower than they would be had you been playing in the morning.

Drainage

Most course designers have incorporated the factor of drainage into their greens when they designed them. When it rains or when the irrigation hits the greens, the water that accumulates needs somewhere to go. Greens are designed to slope to the nearest pond, lake, ocean or drain. When reading greens, look for the drain or the water closest to the edge of the green and use that information to help determine which way gravity will take your ball.

Grain

Grain is a factor that can drive the best players crazy. Understanding the nature of grain is the first lesson in understanding how it affects putts. Simply put, grain is the direction grass grows. Grass doesn't just grow perfectly straight up and down in a vertical line. It bends one way or the other based on the maintenance practices of the golf course. Also, being a plant, grass tends to grow towards the sun wherever it might be at any point during the day. Grain can change from day to day based on many factors. Grain will be more prominent in the south where golf courses have Bermuda grass on the greens as opposed to Bent grass or other northern, cool-weather grasses. Bermuda grass has a thicker, more aggressive growing leaf and will tend to follow the tendencies described earlier more consistently. One of the best places to look for grain on each green is at the edge of the hole. One side of the hole will look like the grass is falling into the hole, where the other side will look like the grass is growing away from the hole. If a ball is rolling with the growing grass, it will travel faster than if it were moving against the growing grass. Often when you are looking into the grain the grass will appear a darker shade of green than if you were looking down grain. Putting to the darker shade will be slower than if you were putting at the shiny, light color green.

If you're still unsure how to read the grain here's a simple secret: use your shadow as a guide. Stand on the green and find your shadow. If your shadow is on your right then the grain should pull your ball to the left. If your shadow is on your left then the grain should pull your ball to the right.

Feel It, See It, Sense It

One of the best ways I like to read greens is by using my feet. I will often walk beside the line of my putt all the way to the hole. Many times my feet will feel something that my eyes can't see. On sharp breaking putts by standing along the line you can get a sense of how severe the slope is and firmness that's in the green.

As you approach the green, whether you are traveling by foot or by golf cart, start your green-reading process. Begin by determining the highest point on the green along with the lowest point on the green. Understand that if you poured a bucket of water on the highest point of the green, it would run to the lowest point. By determining these points on the green you now have a read of which way gravity might try to pull your ball.

Once you are on the green, try to get at least ten feet behind your ball. Crouch down if you can and get your eyes as close to ground level as possible. You don't have to do the Spiderman crouch, like Camilo Ville-gas, but the lower the better. This will help your eyes to have a sense of what direction the green may break. If you aren't getting the feedback and instinctive sense of what the putt may do from behind the ball move to the other side of the hole and have a look from there. While you walk around the hole, be sure to observe the surface of the green from all possible directions for anything that might hint at how your ball will roll.

The main purpose for reading greens is to gain confidence. Confidence in what you are trying to commit to in your putting stroke. It takes a huge amount of trust to commit to something, so the more thorough you are in your read then the more you ought to trust it. If you step up to your putt without being one hundred percent sure of what you want to do with it, your chances of making the putt have just diminished by half. Getting the read right can be difficult; so don't let it frustrate you. Remember, it's better to be decisive than to be right. Your job as a player is to take whatever information you can collect, let your mind and body process it, choose a line you want the ball to take to the hole, and then hit it with your chosen speed. If it goes in, great! If it doesn't, take pride in the fact that you hit the putt exactly how you wanted to and then walk off the green knowing you'll make the next one.

LONG PUTTS
Lag It to Move On

Long putts are never ones that you really look forward to hitting. Although I don't like to talk about the dreaded three-putt, avoiding a three-putt on a very long putt can be round saver. Since making the long putt is more often an accident than skill, try using some mental imagery to lag the first putt close. Imagine a three-foot circle drawn around the hole in white chalk and try to putt the ball inside that circle on your first putt. You'll then have a great chance to make a two putt and move on to the next hole rather than run the risk of an improper read or speed in trying to hole the first putt.

For long putts outside twenty-five feet try reading the putt in two or sometimes even three parts. Split the putt up according to the different parts of the green that it is going to travel through. For example, if the putt begins by going up a steep slope and then flattens out once it is on top of the slope there are two parts for you to consider. First read the part of the putt from the ball to the top of the slope. Next read from just over the crest of the slope to the hole. This will help both with a sense of direction and your sense of feel for the speed. A long putt is rarely a perfectly flat or straight putt.

Always walk off the length of your long putts and pay special attention to what the putt will do the last four or five feet of its roll. By walking off the length of the putt it allows you the opportunity to thoroughly read the green, to see if there's an area around the hole where you would want your ball to end up if you do miss. It also gives you a speed gauge of how hard you'll need to hit the putt according to your memory bank files of past putts of similar lengths.

Once you've gathered all the information needed, make your practice stroke while still looking at the hole. You may want to take a couple extra practice strokes before you go into your routine just to help you feel the length needed for the long putt. In your practice stroke allow your hands to hold the club very lightly; this will help with your feel.

Swing the putter at the same pace the same distance back and through. If you take the putter back too short, or abbreviate your follow through you will cause the ball to jump off line right away and reduce your chance to get it close. With a long stroke it is important to keep the pace constant throughout the stroke. This will keep you from decelerating at impact and the chance of leaving the putt way to short will decrease.

Most amateurs tend to want to look up on long putts, so be sure to keep your head and eyes still in order to hit the putt solidly. If you hit the putt slightly off the heel or off the toe you will lose ten feet or more of distance depending on the overall length of the long putt. Hitting the putt solidly gives you the best chance of accomplishing your goal of two putting and moving on to the next hole.

How to Be a Great Putter

1.ATTITUDE: A great putter is someone with a great attitude about putting. A great putter is someone who can't wait to get to the green to show off what he or she can do with the putter. A great putter is confident, decisive, and accepts the results of every putt no matter what. Regardless of the result, the great putter does the same routine on the next putt.

2.EYES OVER THE BALL: Your eyes need to be over the ball or at least over the target line. This will allow you to see the line of the putt with a simple swivel of the head. It takes two things to make a putt, the right direction and the right distance. When your eyes are over the ball you have the best chance of seeing the correct line, and then putting it down that line. You have eliminated one of the variables for making a putt, now you can concentrate on hitting it the right speed!

3.MIRROR THE BACKSWING & FOLLOW THROUGH: The distance you take the putter back should be the same distance you follow through. If your follow through is shorter than your backswing it probably means you are decelerating into the ball and most likely starting the ball off line. If your backswing is shorter than your follow through then you are most likely steering the ball at your target. The putter should move at the same pace back and through. The pace of the backswing and follow through shouldn't change. There shouldn't be any sudden bursts of energy in the stroke. The more consistent the pace the smoother the stroke and the more consistent the results will be.

4.KEEP A STEADY HEAD: It is true in putting you need to keep your head still, but more importantly keep your eyes still. Don't let your eyes follow the putter head away from the ball. Keep your eyes focused on one spot on the ball. I recommend the back of the ball but I have seen many good players focus on many different spots of the ball. Imagine someone is standing in front of you holding your head as you putt. Your shoulders and arms are the main source of movement in your putting stroke. Don't let your hands and wrists control what the putter head does. You don't want the hands and wrists locked up so they create tension just not controlling the action. Your shoulders and arms should act together working at the same speed the entire stroke.

5.BELIEF IN YOURSELF: A great putter believes they are going to make every putt. They wouldn't go as far as to bet their homes on any given putt, but at the same time they have a quiet confidence about their ability to make putts, and more importantly they have a great attitude about themselves. When they miss it's never them, it's a spike mark, the green or the putter.

THE TOP 5 PUTTING DRILLS

1. CHALK LINE DRILLS:
a. Six Feet and In: Put a chalk line down on a straight putt. Set a tee at 3 feet, 4 feet, and 5 feet and 6 feet. Using four balls, putt 12 putts from each tee or station. Count the amount of makes. Repeat this until you make them all, or beat your personal best.

b. The ladder drill: Set up a chalk line on a straight putt. Set tees at 3 feet, 4 feet, 5 feet, and 6 feet. Using four balls put one ball at each station. Starting from the 3 feet station continue up the "ladder" and repeat until you miss. Set a goal for makes in-a-row, or beat your personal best. Plan on being there all day!

c. Coin and Putter: Depending on what type of putter you use, put a coin (nickel, dime, or penny) on the back of your putter. The coin should be far enough on to be balanced. Putt 10, 3 foot putts, 10, 4 foot putts, and 10 5 foot putts keeping the coin on the back of the putter at least until impact. This will help ensure a smooth transition from the backswing to the downswing. This drill will force your stroke to be the same pace back and through.

2. BALLS IN A CIRCLE DRILL: Use 7 balls. Put the balls in a circle around the hole, each ball should be three feet from the hole and evenly spaced from each other. When you make all seven balls without missing in one circle around, move to a four foot circle. Repeat with five foot circle and six foot circle.

3. PUTT TO THE FRINGE AND NEVER MISS DRILL: When working on controlling your distance putt from fringe to fringe. Pick areas of the fringe where you are trying to get your ball to stop. The "perfect" putt will be one that ends up leaning against the fringe. You are working on distance control and not missing any putts while doing so. Therefore you aren't damaging your confidence by missing putt after putt.

4. PUTT WITH EYES CLOSED—LISTENING DRILL: Using four balls start at four feet, go through your putting routine, and at the last second before you start your stroke close your eyes. Stroke the putt and listen for the ball to go in the hole. This will teach you to trust the feel of your stroke and also to keep your head and eyes still long after you have stroked the putt. You can also try this in your practice rounds.

5. PUTT AND STEP BACK: Pick a particular break either a left to right break or a right to left break. Start in gimmie range to make your first putt. Then step back on the same line and putt again. If you make it then you get to step back again but if you miss you must start over. See how far back you can go before you over or under putt the break and miss. Watch each putt as it takes the break and memorize what speed was needed on each length. Put that valuable information in your memory bank for future use. My personal record to date is 25 steps back. Beat that!

The Best Putting Games

1. RAPID FIRE: This is a 2-person game. Using two holes, you each start at opposite holes. You will both putt at the same time. If one player makes and the other misses, the player making will receive a point and then the players switch holes. If both players make, no points are given and the players both stay at the same hole. If neither player makes,

you retrieve the opponent's ball and putt immediately. The winner is the first one to hole five putts. (The game is meant to be a fast paced game and played with a putt of about 10-15 feet. This will encourage a lot of makes. The purpose for the game is to take your mind off the mechanics of putting and get it into the thought of just stroking the putt without thinking.)

2. 21: This is a 2-person game. Using two holes anywhere from 15-30 feet apart. Players will begin at the same hole. If you make the putt it counts as five points, lip-outs count as three points, and the closest to the hole counts as one point. Determine who goes first and play whoever wins more points on each hole has honors from that point on. The first player to 21 without going over 21 wins. If you go over 21 you immediately go back to 13 points. There are no stymies in the game, you may mark a ball to move it out of the way of the next putter. (The game will allow you to follow your routine and get you in the mindset of making putts.)

3. THE LOOP MATCH: Most putting greens have anywhere from 3 to 18 holes cut for practice putting holes. Use every hole and follow the outside perimeter of holes. Play stroke or match play (depending on the number of players) and play by the rules of golf. It always makes a match a little more interesting if you put a little wager of some sort on it. Maybe a soda or a golf ball. (This game will get you competing in a game-like situation. It is different putting against an opponent when it means something. This will make your heart beat a little faster and get your competitive juices flowing. Putting in a real round is different from the practice green or playing by yourself.)

4. SAFETY DRAWBACK: As many players as you want can play, no more than four recommended. Competitors will alternate picking holes to putt to. If your putt doesn't travel at least the distance to the hole, the player must pull the ball back one putter length away from the hole from where the ball ended up. Also, if the player hits the putt further by the hole than "inside the leather" he/she must also pull the ball one-putter length away from the hole from where the ball ended up. Players will play a nine-hole match to determine the winner. (This game puts a premium on distance control but still forces you to make good solid strokes under the pressure of playing against someone.)

CHAPTER SUMMARY:
ESSENTIALS FOR PLAYING SCRATCH GOLF
PUTTING

➤All great putters have two things in common. 1. They get their eyes directly over the target line. 2. They swing the putter head back and through the same distance.

➤Swinging the putter back and through at the same pace will help eliminate any "jerky" or quick movements in the stroke that can get the ball rolling off line in a hurry.

➤In your putting set up, be comfortable. If you aren't comfortable it creates tension and tension takes away your ability to swing the putter freely.

➤Develop a routine, both mental and physical that can be repeated time and time again in every situation. Your routine is up to you, and should most definitely have something in it that personalizes it to you. The key to a good routine is your ability to execute it exactly the same on every putt. Here are key components of a solid routine:

➤A Trigger Point, or Starting Point

➤A Decisive, Committed Approach

➤Comfortable Set Up

➤A Last Look At The Target

➤Reading greens is more of an art than it is a science. Use your instincts and imagination to "feel" what a putt does. Always trust your read. Don't forget the following tips for reading greens:

➤Use your feet to help with the read… walk the line of the putt to the hole

➤Begin reading the green well before you reach the green

➤Find the high point and the low point on the green

➤Read the putt from at least 10 feet behind the ball

➤Remember that you are reading the putt in order to gain confidence in what you are trying to commit to. Be 100% sure of you read when you approach the putt

➤For long putts, divide the putt into two or three parts and read each part separately
➤Keep your head AND your eyes still during every stroke

➤Your shoulders and arms are the main source of movement in the putting stroke

➤Your attitude will determine whether or not you are going to make or miss putts. Attitude is the single most important part of putting. You choose your attitude.

JUNIOR GOLFERS PUTTING ESSENTIALS:

➤Keep putting simple. Take a picture of the hole with your eyes and see the picture while you are putting

➤Make putting fun. Play games with your friends and challenge yourself to become a great putter. Remember, Great Golfers are Great Putters!

➤Putt to the sides of the green and not always to the hole. See if you can get your ball to stop on the edge of the green five times in a row… then ten… then fifteen…

TOURNAMENT PLAYERS PUTTING ESSENTIALS:

➤Six feet and closer is where you need to be deadly. 80% of your putting practice should be from six feet and closer.

➤Find someone to play putting games with to put pressure on yourself.

➤Make putting a game within the game. Enjoy the opportunity to putt.

➤Too many players allow putting to "get in their head" and ruin the chance to become a great competitive player. Make the choice that you aren't going to let this happen to you. Work on the fundamentals spelled out in this chapter and develop the attitude that you are a GREAT putter.

PUTTING… The Great Equalizer

➤Putting puts men, women, and children on the same playing field. The thoughts, ideas, and techniques aren't age or gender bias.

➤Putting takes little strength or athletic ability

➤Great Putting takes attitude and confidence which can be adapted by anyone

CHAPTER

3

The Short Game

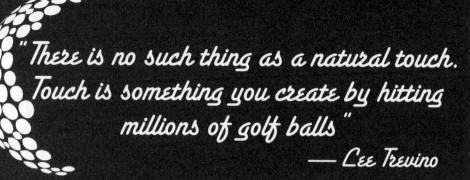

"There is no such thing as a natural touch. Touch is something you create by hitting millions of golf balls"
— Lee Trevino

THE BREAD AND BUTTER OF A CHAMPION

Any good golfer will tell you that mistakes made from the tee to the green can be set right if you have a great short game. You can be hitting your long game shots bad all day but with the proper attitude, mental toughness and a solid short game you can still post a good score for the round.

Many amateur golfers don't see the importance of the short game. They relate their final score to how many times they didn't hit the driver perfect or how often they didn't hit it on the green on the approach shot. No one will argue that golf becomes easier when you hit it in the fairway and on the greens in regulation, but I don't think many will argue that hitting every green and every fairway is quite unlikely through the course of eighteen holes. Having a mental toughness about you and an attitude that you are going to get the ball in the hole no matter what will not only save you shots, but it will make you a champion.

Playing a practice round on a typical winter day in Florida, there was a stiff east wind coming off the Atlantic Ocean for my second shot on a long par-5 hole. My opponents had both chose to lay up on this par 5 in which water guards the last 70 yards short of the green. I had driven the ball well and had just 220 yards left to the hole and 215 yards to carry the water. I chose 3- iron for the shot which if hit well would be plenty of club to reach the green. I made what felt like my second swing of the day (because it was) and I pushed the ball badly to the right where it continued to soar with the wind pushing it even further right. The ball was flying so far right I found myself rooting it on with the hopes that it would land past the pond to the right possibly giving me the chance to play it without taking a penalty stroke. The ball disappeared behind the large palm trees that framed the edge of the hole.

I jumped in the cart and anxiously drove down the fairway and toward the next shot. To my delight I found the ball on dry land to the right of the pond just as I had hoped. It was inside the hazard line but playable. I was left with a severe downhill stance and a buried lie in thick Bermuda rough. The pin was cut just over the six or seven paces on the green. About ten paces beyond the hole, a deep pot bunker with soft sand and a sure downhill lie. The total distance of the shot was about 25 yards. My opponents each hit their third shots on the green within 15 feet of the hole, so the decision was simple. I needed to be aggressive with the shot and hit it at the flag. I pulled my 60-degree wedge out of my bag and started to get a feel for the downhill lie and also the thickness of the grass just outside of the hazard line. I took a few practice swings trying to feel the angle at which I wanted the clubface to strike the ball. I checked the wind, which was the only positive aspect; it was directly in my face, which would allow me to be more aggressive. I took a wider than normal stance, angled my shoulders with the downhill slope, and took two slow backswings trying to emulate the backswing I wanted to execute. I took a deep breath, looked one more time at my target, back at the ball, and with soft hands I took the club back. A long backswing, fully under control transitioned to a mighty downswing. In the blink of an eye I heard, "plunk," my ball flopped in the water about ten yards in front of me.

I couldn't believe that I had just done that. I felt perfect before and during the shot. I had ultimate confidence that I was going to hit a great shot, I was sure of it. Since I was in a hazard I realized I had misjudged the lie, which couldn't be checked under the rules of golf. It was a little thicker and softer than I anticipated. I was disappointed, but not ready to give up. Preparing for the initial shot over the water I had been taking practice swings not far from my drop point and was confident that I could still hit a good shot. I pulled another Titleist from my bag and made the drop. I took a couple more practice swings and focused intensely on the spot I wanted my ball to land. I took my stance, again wider than normal, tilted my shoulders forward to help feel the slope of the hill, relaxed my hands and took one last peak at the flag. I took what felt like the same backswing and came down and through the ball with soft, aggressive hands. The contact with the ball was crisp and soft at the same time. I finished balanced and with my hands controlled and high. I looked up just in time to see the ball bounce on the green in the exact spot I had envisioned. It took one bounce, checked back with some spin and gently rolled into the hole. My opponents gasped! Suddenly they realized they had to hole their putts otherwise the sure win would turn into a "halve" in the match shifting confidence and momentum in my direction.

This story is an example of how resilience, a never-give-up attitude and an arsenal of short game shots can always keep you in the hole. It also proves that you never know when the right attitude, acceptance of your shots, and a great short game can save you throughout a round or a tournament. If you can learn to approach your short game with a positive, can-do attitude you will find yourself hitting more and more successful short game shots.

THE CHIP SHOT

Once you have established the chipping basics and good fundamental technique, the battle of chipping becomes easier, and much more fun. One aspect that you need to be aware of about short game shots is that no shot is exactly the same. Around the greens the shots become trickier because of the many different lies, the shorter distances and the varying speeds in which you have to swing the club. Even though many of these short shots require some imagination you can be sure that all short shots around the green evolve from the fundamentals of one basic shot: the chip shot.

The definition of the chip shot is: A shot in which the ball spends more time on the ground than in the air.

To better visualize the chip shot, imagine you have just come up short of the green with your approach shot. The pin is cut in the front part of the green, your ball is twenty feet from the hole and just four feet from the green's surface there is a sprinkler head blocking the green. If you were to use your putter it would have to be hit around the sprinkler head giving you no chance at making the shot unless you are willing to chance a bad bounce from the sprinkler head. Not an option if you are attacking the golf course, as you should be, so the shot required is a slightly lofted club, maybe an eight or nine iron, to get the ball in the air for that three or four feet where the sprinkler head sits waiting to affect the outcome.

CHIP SHOT FUNDAMENTALS

Grip

In the basic chip shot you want your grip to be the same as your putting grip. The fundamentals of the putting grip will keep the grip closer to the palm of your hand helping to eliminate the hinging motion in the stroke. Remember, you won't be hitting the ball very far in the basic chip shot so much like with the putter, the softer you hold your hands the more touch and feel you will have. The most important aspect of the grip is for you to be able to reduce the amount of hand action during the shot.

Grip the chip like a putting grip to reduce rotation

Grip the club down on the handle about two inches above the point where the handle ends and the steel or graphite of the shaft becomes exposed. This allows for maximum control of the club during the stroke.

Stance & Posture

The stance for the chip shot needs to be narrow with just 6 to 8 inches separating your feet. It is not necessary to have a wide stance because there is no force behind the stroke of the chip that you need to support. The stance should also be open to the target line, meaning it should be aimed about 30 degrees to the left (for a right handed golfer) of the target. This allows the thighs and the hips to be out of the way while you are swinging the club and it limits the motion your arms and shoulders need to make.

Take a narrow, open stance and lean towards the target

The posture of the chip shot begins, once again, at the hips. Begin your posture with the hips pushing back directly away from the ball. Your torso will then bend down towards the ball and your arms should hang freely and comfortably from the shoulders. The knees must be flexed slightly but just enough so that they feel light and ready. Its important that your legs do not feel locked with tension and a lack of movement.

Good chipping posture with the hips pushed away from the ball, slight knee flex, a slightly open stance, and leaning towards the target

Ball Position

Ball position is where the amateur player struggles the most on the chip shot. The ball should be placed slightly back of center for the basic chip shot. It is critical to the consistency of this shot to hit down on the ball and by having the ball behind the bottom of the pendulum of this shot will help encourage the downward blow you are looking for on the chip.

Play the ball in the back part of your stance

Too far forward will cause all kinds of un-wanted problems

LEAN FOR STABILITY

Since this is such a short shot there doesn't need to be any extra movement or swaying. Lean your torso towards the target once you have set your posture and taken your stance to stabilize the balance of your entire body. You want to feel 75% of your total weight on your left side if you are a right-handed golfer. You will find when you lean the torso at the target; the hips and legs will naturally follow the angle of the torso and will then set the lower body still.

The proper lean is balanced throughout the body   If the hips get in front of the body trouble begins

Leaning the torso will also give way to the feeling of a descending blow on the ball. With the body angled toward the ground, this will give you a great feel of hitting down on the back of the ball promoting better contact and more consistently.

PICK A SPOT & SEE THE SHOT!

The chip shot is similar to the putt in that you need to have a good picture of the shot in your mind before it happens. You'll want to incorporate the same fundamentals of reading greens that you use during putting, whenever you are chipping, because after all, you are trying to make the chip. The first thing to plan out is how the ball will react once it hits the green. Keep in mind that the ball's bounce will react based on the trajectory, the wind conditions, and the uphill or downhill landing areas. When you are picturing the shot, visualize precisely what the ball will do when it lands on the green.

Once you have visualized what the ball will do, choose a specific spot on the green where you want your ball to land. The more exact this spot is and the more you can focus intently on that spot will determine the more likely you will be able to hit your ball to that spot. If you can learn to control your mind to think only of that spot where you want the ball to land then you will help eliminate all the mechanical and technical thoughts that tend to produce poor chip shots. Once your chip shot routine begins, your mind should never waiver from you thinking only of the target you are trying to hit. The better you become at creating a mental picture of your ball traveling towards the target, on your chosen line and hitting your spot, then the greater your chances of that exact picture happening will become.

Pick out a Perfect landing spot

Dotted line of balls on green, indicates the landing spot and then the path the ball will take to the hole

THE CHIP ROUTINE

Once you have visualized the shot needed for your chip then follow this routine:

1.Be sure you are holding the club as softly as you can. There is no room for tension in your hands, wrists or arms.

2.Position the ball in the back of a narrow stance.

3.Open your stance to the target line. This will help you to see the target, the line and will also give you the feeling of swinging your arms and shoulders. Opening your body will keep you from creating any resistance from your body, which would inhibit your chip.

4.Keep your chin up and out of your chest and your back straight.

5.Focus solely on the landing spot you have picked out and lean forward on the swing.

HAVE A CLOCK'S TEMPO: TICK-TOCK!

The chipping stroke, like the putting stroke, does not require strength to execute the shot. It is a two-part action that is mainly controlled by the shoulders. The hands and arms are simply support for the greater part of the stroke. There doesn't need to be much force in the shot because the ball will only be in the air for less than ten feet. The main goal in the chipping stroke is to hit the ball solidly, making sure that the club is traveling downward when it strikes the ball and in order to do that you must have good tempo.

When working on tempo, start the backswing with your shoulders. The hands and arms will then follow what the shoulders initiate. Don't let your arms separate too far from your body or you'll lose the feeling of the pendulum that you want to have throughout the stroke. Take the club back and through with good tempo, much like the rhythm of a clock: tick-tock, tick-tock. This, clock rhythm, is a simple way to think of the tempo you want during the entire chipping stroke. There should be no thoughts or sense of quickness or speed in the shot, as you will want to keep the backswing and forward swing the same length with a consistent tempo throughout.

The stroke should go back and through the same distance

Along with good tempo on the shot, you want to insure that you make a descending blow on the ball. In other words, hit down on it! The stroke itself may be short, but you don't want to stab at the ball either. Always make sure you are accelerating through the ball. The hands should, at some point, return to where they began the shot, which means that the hands will never get in front of the club head before impact. The only way this can happen is if the wrist collapses and you flip the club head through the impact position.

Flipping the club is the cardinal sin of chipping

The flipping of the wrists is the most common mistake made with the chipping stroke. You will struggle to develop any consistency in your chips if you are constantly flipping your wrists. This error comes from a conscious or sub-conscious thought that you need to help the ball into the air by scooping it up. This scooping action happens when you uncock your wrists on the downswing, which means the hands are now moving faster than the arms and shoulders which then creates too much speed with the club head and allows it to get to the ball much too early in the stroke. Not only does the club head arrive too early, but it is usually on the upswing by the time it reaches the ball, which will often cause the dreaded Vince Skully or thin shot that goes sailing across the green. This same scooping motion is also the cause for the ole chilly-dipper or fat shot as well. These are two chipping mistakes that will kill your confidence and your score.

Taking into consideration the length of the shot you are hitting, it is OK to hinge your wrists a little bit on the way back. The longer the shot the more you may need to hinge but just make sure on the way back to the ball, your hands are leading the club head.

Don't let the club head lead the hands...   Let the hands lead the club head

If you can slow down the hands and start the downswing with the shoulders the release of the club head will happen naturally and you won't need to consciously think about it.

WHICH CLUB?

You have fourteen clubs in your bag to choose from, when it comes time to chip so it is important that you choose the right one for the shot you are attempting. Understand that each club when using the exact same chipping stroke under the exact same conditions will produce a different shot. The less lofted clubs such as a seven or eight iron with a medium length stroke at a medium speed pace will create a shot where the ball spends very little time in the air and potentially a good distance relative to the shot on the surface, rolling to the target. A more lofted club like a sand wedge or a lob wedge with a medium length and medium pace stroke will cause the ball to pop up in the air but will fly approximately the same distance as the seven or eight iron. However; because of the loft of the club the ball will not roll as far. It is a good rule to follow that the longer the distance to the hole, the less lofted club you should use. The shorter the distance the more likely you will need a more lofted club. Each situation and every shot will require something different. You always need to judge the lie, the wind, the read of the green, and of course the situation you are in before choosing a club.

Most players will gravitate to one or two of their favorite chipping clubs every time. The choice is likely due to the simple fact that they practice more with these clubs and have that extra confidence needed in the pressure situations of the short game. Having more club choices is always better but that of course means that you must be equally rehearsed for each club choice. When you are well rehearsed with many different clubs you will often know the shot you are supposed to hit as soon as you walk up to your ball.

Choose the right club for the shot

As it is with all shots in golf you want to approach each shot with the ultimate commitment to the shot. Arriving at this commitment requires the ability to have the confidence in the shot you have selected and the club you have chosen to hit the shot. It is important for you to go out and practice with each club to find out which shots you can hit with each. You need to know which club you are more comfortable with from close distances and what you will use from a distance much further away. What you will use out of deep rough and what you would do from a thin lie. Practicing for each situation is the only way you will find out which club you have the most confidence in when you are chipping.

A ROUGH SITUATION

When you are in heavy rough around the green the grass will have the tendency to grab the clubface and de-loft it, so using a more lofted club than normal is the way to combat the grabby tendencies. Even if the grass does take some of the loft off the club, the shot can still act like a chip shot from using the more lofted club. When making a shot out of thick rough it will require that you use a more pronounced set up position. Hold the club more firmly as this will aid in keeping the clubface more square through impact. Keep in mind the thick grass will try to turn the club as it moves toward the ball so the angle of attack should be more of a V-shape swing with a greater downward action. As you start your shoulders in the beginning of the stroke, hinge the wrists more abruptly than you normally would. This will help to create the steeper angle needed for the down swing. Keep the wrists firm like the regular chipping stroke and focus primarily on hitting down on the ball. The more abrupt the angle of attack, the less likely the grass will be to catch the club head. Also be sure to abbreviate the follow through to encourage maximum speed of the stroke at impact.

Out of deep rough exaggerate the set up, take a steep backswing and an abrupt downswing with an abbreviated follow through

TOP 5 CHIPPING DRILLS

1. ONE- HANDED DRILL: Chip balls to a middle-range chipping distance using just the left hand. Put your right hand behind your back and set up to the chip shot with only your left hand on the club. Hit ten shots to the target. What you are gaining by doing this is a feel for the purpose of the left hand and arm during the chip. You will notice that if the left wrist allows the hand to release the club too early you will feel the affects of the scooping motion. Next, put your left hand behind your back and set up to the chip with just your right hand on the club. Hit ten balls to the same middle-range chipping target. By doing this you will soon feel the purpose of the right hand in the chip shot. You may also find that your right hand could be the reason for that dreaded scooping motion in your chip shots. Finally, finish the drill by chipping ten balls with both hands lightly on the club using perfect tempo. After using only one hand for the twenty previous shots, you will begin to feel how your hands need to work together during the chip shot.

2. OVER YOUR BAG: Put your golf bag no more than five feet in front of you between you and the nearest edge of the green. Next, choose a club that will allow you to chip the ball over the bag but will not fly the ball more than two feet past the edge of the green. Next, put a tee in line with the direction you are chipping at that point no more than two feet on the green to indicate a shot that travels too far in the air. Count out ten balls and chip the ten balls over your bag trying to land each ball short of the spot you chose no more than two feet on the green. When you chip all ten for a perfect score, change distances from the bag. You may need to choose a different club once you change distances to make the shot work. You will soon begin to develop a feel for which clubs you hit higher and lower and also the speed in which you need to swing to make a perfect shot.

3. DIFFERENT WEAPONS DRILL: Take out your 7 iron, 8 iron, 9 iron, all the wedges in your bag and five golf balls. Pick a relatively simple chip of medium distance. Start with your seven iron and chip all five balls to the same target then pick up the balls and from the same spot, use your 8 iron to chip to the same target. Take notice of which club produced more consistent results. Continue this process for each club. When you are finished you will see which one or two clubs are best suited to make that particular shot. Now change the shot and do it all again... and again... and again... and again.

4. 9-BALL DRILL: Take one golf ball, your favorite chipping club, and your putter to the practice green. The drill is for you to drop the ball nine times in nine different positions and try to get up and down. Be sure to drop in different lies: downhill, uphill, rough, fairway, close to the green, a little further from the green, etc...for each shot. After you make each chip, take your putter and see if you can make the putt. When you get up-and-down for all nine holes, change to a different chipping club and do it all again.

5. PRACTICE THE MUST MAKE! As you improve your chipping, your goal should change from just getting it close, to making your chips. You attitude needs to be similar to your putting where you believe you are going to make the shot. Find a simple chip shot and take your favorite chipping club, or the club you feel most confident that you can make the chip. Chip balls until you make at least one chip. The confidence that is gained from holing a chip is unmatched. Pick a number under ten and stay until you make that number of chips. As you improve, challenge yourself with a more difficult chip but don't get too crazy... the idea is to get used to holing your chip shots!

THE PITCH SHOT

The pitch shot is different from the chip shot in many ways and at the same time it is similar. You will notice that as you move further and further away from the hole the strokes and swing you use all seem to evolve from each other. Just as the chipping stroke was a lengthened version of the putting stroke, the pitch shot is an off-take of the chip shot expanding on the fundamental set-up and the technique of the stroke itself.

The definition of the pitch shot is just the opposite of the chip shot. Remember the definition of the chip shot says that the ball spends more time on the ground than in the air. Conversely the pitch shot spends more time in the air than on the ground. Consider for a moment what it takes to force the ball to spend more time in the air than on the ground. Clearly the technique of the shot will require a motion that would favor popping the ball in the air. Most likely the club you are going to chose will have more loft and considering the time the ball spends in the air, there will need to be additional speed created during the shot. Although the pitch shot is not a long shot, the movement of the arms, shoulders, and hands needs to be greatly increased making the technique critical.

The pitch shot is fundamentally a miniature version of your full golf swing except the set up position needs to be adjusted to start you in the position that will give you the best chance to make the motions necessary to hit a soft, lofted, and controlled pitch shot. Go through the fundamentals as you have with putting, the chip and your full swing.

PITCH SHOT FUNDAMENTALS

Grip

The grip used for a pitch shot is the same as that of your full swing. It is important to get the grip in the fingers so that the hands and body can work together to release the club. Like the full grip, the handle of the club should pass along the pads of the fingers on the left hand beginning at the base of the right forefinger and exiting the left hand (assuming a right handed golfer) just below the pad below the pinkie finger on the left hand.

The left hand should be in a strong position for a pitch shot. This will help to hinge the hands abruptly after take-away. Strengthening the left hand means you will turn the left hand further to the right, or on top of the club.

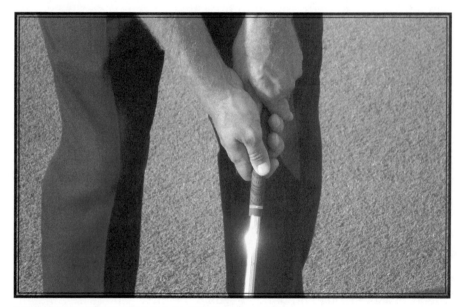

A strong grip allows the wrists to help in the pitch shot

Your right hand fits on the club the same as when you take your grip for a full shot. If you overlap, interlock, or use a ten-finger grip then do the same for the pitch shot. Naturally the right hand grip is going to fit on the handle slightly strong to match the strengthened left hand but the most important factor is to have the two hands working together to hinge and unhinge the wrists.

Posture & Stance

Setting up to the pitch shot is similar to that of the chip shot. The length of the shot will determine some of the factors in the set up but the stance remains narrow and open. The feet should be just a few inches wide from instep to instep for shorter pitch shots and for the longer pitch shots that will require a longer more aggressive swing, the stance will need to be widened some for stability.

Narrow the stance for shorter pitch shots and widen it for longer shots

The posture begins from the hips. Bending from the hips will create the athletic feel needed to allow for the various movements, the control of balance and the speed of the shot. Keeping the back straight is critical in helping bring the club head back to the ball more consistently and so that you can make a balanced attack on the ball. A comfortable knee flex will help you to get down to the ball without reaching and that should give you the feeling of being light on your feet as well as flexible.

Good posture from the profile position looking down the target line from behind

Ball Position

The ball position for the pitch should be further forward in the stance than in the chip shot. Determining how much loft you will need to have on the pitch shot is part of the feel you must have from hours of practice. By moving the ball further forward in your stance while keeping all other parts in the same place you will naturally increase the loft on the club. Keep in mind that the more loft you choose to put on the club being used, the more aggressive the shot needs to be in order to create the speed necessary to propel the ball the correct distance.

The further forward the ball is in the stance naturally the more loft is put on the club allowing for higher trajectory on the shot

STILL LEAN

The weight distribution at the address position should be favoring the target side. At address the torso leans towards the target giving you the feeling of having your weight up to 70% on the left side. Although the weight shifts slightly during the stroke, leaning still gives you the feel of returning to the left side throughout the stroke. The other important benefit of leaning towards the target is that it promotes a steeper arc, which will promote a more solid contact of the ball.

Lean toward the target at set up to promote a descending hit on the ball

The shoulders create the angle of attack

PITCH IT OR CHIP IT

Imagine yourself on a basketball court with a basketball in your hand and Michael Jordan standing at the free throw line at the far end of the court. If your life depended on you throwing the ball from the spot you are standing to Mr. Jordan on the other side of the court which method do you think you would use to get the ball to him? You could toss the ball a short distance in the air and then have it roll in a straight line all the way down the floor or you could rare-back and throw it like a baseball and attempt to fly it the entire way down to the other end of the court. In this visualization, it is clear that by rolling the ball to the other end of the court, it would take far less strength and less athletic ability to get it there. Tossing the ball the length of the court would require great precision, strength, and the correct touch of how hard you need to throw it.

Now think about the same two options from Michael Jordan's perspective. If the ball is thrown like a baseball, and assuming it is a good throw he would be able to stand in one place with very little movement, reach his hands out in front of him and catch the high, soft pass. If the ball is rolled along the ground he would have to change his stance, bend down to pick it up, secure it, and then stand back up returning to the position he started from.

The chip shot versus the pitch shot is similar to this hypothetical visualization. Like rolling the ball across the basketball court, the chip shot is a much higher percentage shot that requires less movement and is much easier to predict the shot outcome. The pitch shot which is similar to throwing the basketball the length of the floor requires much more strength, accuracy, and touch. In summary, the athletic requirement is much greater for the pitch shot than for the chip shot.

As pointed out earlier, the pitch shot is a mini version of the full golf swing. The difference is in the length of the swing and in the tapered down motion of the moving body parts. Within this reduced version of the swing the lower body plays an important role. The hips turn back slightly as the shoulders start the swing.

The hips turn back slightly while the shoulders make a good turn to start the shot

There needs to be a balance of enough movement to increase the speed of the club head proportional to the length of the shot you are attempting to be hit. Enough momentum needs to be created in order to slide the club under the ball and through the grass but not too much so as to cause the ball to fly past the target.

The pitch begins by choosing the proper loft needed to hit the shot. Proper club choice begins the process and continues with choosing the proper ball position, hand position, and placement of the club. The lob wedge is the club in your bag with the most loft. Just like on the chip shot, if you want to manipulate the loft then open the clubface by moving the ball forward in your stance or keep your hands even with the ball.

Your hands play a major role in the pitch shot. It is critical to hold the club lightly and at the same time insure a sharp hinging motion. Picking the club upward will cause the hands to hinge naturally. The length of the swing will depend on the length of the shot. Regardless of the length of the shot, it is always important to have good tempo in the stroke. The hips should move in sequence with the shoulders, arms, and hands while finishing balanced and firm over the left side.

The hands hinge on the way back and hold the angle through impact to maintain the loft of the club

In the downswing of the pitch shot your main objective is to slide the club head under the ball while being sure to accelerate. DO NOT rotate or release the club head in dramatic fashion during the downswing or this will shut the clubface and deloft the club. On the follow through keep the clubface pointing towards the sky to show that you have maintained the proper loft.

THE PARTIAL WEDGE SHOT

A long pitch shot is one of the toughest shots in golf. Just as the pitch shot is a miniature version of the full swing, the partial pitch is even more of a hybrid that moves further away from the technique of the chip and pitch shot and moves closer to the fundamentals of the full swing. The in-between manner of this shot makes the timing and the tempo of the stroke, one of the toughest to control.

This is a shot that you will certainly encounter in almost every round of golf you play. For you amateur golfers, this might be a shot you will need to hit after having hit a tee shot in the woods and then punching out to 30 or 40 yards. For you tournament players, this might be an opportunity to make a birdie on a par-5 hole if you don't quite reach the green on your second shot. Either way, the partial wedge shot is a must have shot in order to move you closer to playing scratch golf so let's go through the fundamentals of this shot.

Grip

For the partial wedge shot you want to grip the club using the same grip that you would use for your full golf swing. This shot requires a combined technique of the full swing and the pitch shot and because of that you want to have that same freedom to use your hands as used in the pitch shot all while using the basic technique of your full swing. In a 40-yard wedge shot, the hands are not the focal point for creating the speed needed but at the same time, restricting them would make it difficult to feel the shot as needed. It's that combination of the feel and freedom in your hands and your full swing that makes or breaks this shot.

Posture & Stance

The stance is the beginning point of the blend in the partial wedge shot. The stance needs to be a little bit wider than that of a pitch shot, but still more narrow than that of a your full swing. The feet should be aligned slightly open, more conducive to what the basic pitch shot calls for.

Set up for a pitch shot

Set up for a full swing

Set up for a partial wedge is a hybrid of the full swing and the pitch shot

The posture again begins with the hips pointing down toward the ball. It is imperative for the lower body to act as a stable base for the upper body to work around. You want to have the feeling of peaking over the edge of a cliff in order to get the weight of your torso leaning forward. This position with the torso will allow you to rotate the body in the core area and control the overall pace of the shot, which is critical to its execution. Most importantly you should feel comfortable and light on your feet for this shot. Although it doesn't require the athleticism of the full swing, this partial wedge shot does require that you to have full control of the movement of your entire body throughout the entire stroke.

Ball Position

The ball position for the partial wedge shot is slightly back of the center of your stance. This position will enable you to retain the feeling of hitting down on the ball and at the same time it will give you enough room to be aggressive through the ball. If the ball position is too far back in your stance you will have the feel of chopping at the ball. If you have it too far forward in your stance you will run the risk of hitting the ball on the upswing, which will produce inconsistent results.

The ball too far back in the stance creates a trapping motion

The ball too far forward can lead to a skulled shot

USE THE MUSCLES, NOT THE HANDS

Make sure the chest and shoulders start the swing. Take the club away, low and straight away from the ball. The hips should then follow what the hands and arms are doing but shouldn't become too active during the backswing. Hinge the wrists slightly on the takeaway but certainly don't cock them to full potential. The hands should feel free, yet controlled and partnered with the motions of the body.

The hips lead the downswing

Notice in the picture that the hips lead the downswing with the shoulders and chest following. You should never start the return to the ball with just your arms and hands because the arms and hands if working separately from the rest of the body will make it much too difficult to regulate the club-head speed and loft of the club through impact. Thinking of unwinding the hips while letting your arms and hands follow along will give you the proper control of your torso, which will allow for a controlled and abbreviated finish. If you are able to abbreviate the finish it will then prove to you that you have allowed your big muscles to control the motion through the stroke and not the hands.

The variety of shots that you can hit by mastering this technique is virtually endless. Simply by changing ball position, loft of club, or both you can hit higher and softer shots or lower running shots of various distances within the partial wedge range.

TOP 5 WEDGE DRILLS

1. PERFECT THE BACKSWING/CONTROL THE DOWNSWING— Put yourself into the proper backswing position and hold it there to start the shot. Begin the downswing focusing solely on the movement of the hips while feeling the arms, hands, and shoulders chasing the movement of the hips. Notice the faster you move the hips, the further the ball will travel.

2. DISTANCE CONTROL DRILL— Set piles of ten balls 30, 40, and 50 yards from the same target. Start at the 30-yard pile and hit one ball. Go through your routine just like you would during an important round or match. Move to the 40-yard shot, go through your routine, and hit the shot to the same target. Move to the 50-yard shot and repeat the process. Stay at the 50-yard shot and follow the same process. Work your way through all 3 piles one shot at a time. After you have hit the 30 balls, take note of the pattern of your shots. If the majority of your misses are in a consistent pattern you will need to make the proper adjustments next time through.

3. 15 BALL DRILL—Use 15 balls from the same spot and hit to three different partial wedge distances. Hit shots alternating between the three distances. On the first round of three hit all regular shots. The next time, hit all three shots on a low trajectory by moving the ball slightly back in your stance and possibly using a less lofted club. The third time through, hit all three of the shots on a higher than normal trajectory by moving the ball slightly forward and possibly using a more lofted club. Take notice of which shots you hit more crisply and use the last two rounds to work on your less productive shots. Always go through your routine, as you would do on the golf course.

4. PITCHING H-O-R-S-E—Take a small basket of range balls and a friend and go out on the course. Play a short game skills game of horse

with the only requirement is that your pitch must be hit over something before landing on the green. Whoever hits the ball furthest from the flag is penalized a letter until one person spells horse. Examples: Over the golf cart at the flag. Over the tree at the flag.

5. 3 GREENS— Divide a green into three sections by laying down clubs as dividers and then number each section. Go out to 50-yards and practice hitting into each section of the green by calling out a section number and then hitting into it. Stay until you can hit each section on command.

THE FLOPPER

I remember as a kid watching the Skins Game on Thanksgiving weekend. One of my most vivid memories of the Skins Game was watching Freddie Couples hit a towering high soft shot from about twenty-five feet off the green, out of the rough, and over a bunker. The shot appeared impossible and the commentators on TV were predicting sure failure. He took a violent swing that resembled the power I would have put into my long drive contest swing. The ball took off straight up in the air and seemed to stay there for four or five seconds. In the next blink the ball landed two feet from the hole, jumped forward a foot and stopped just 12 inches from the hole. I was wowed by the shot... and so were the television announcers. Shortly after Couples hit that shot on the telecast they replayed the shot in slow motion. What appeared at first to be a violent swing with no control and a lot of luck turned into a controlled work of art with an incredible amount of touch.

I was once told by one of my first teachers that touch was just another word for talent. He claimed if you didn't have the talent then you shouldn't be trying to hit shots like the flop shot, which require a tremendous amount of touch and feel. Since then, I am confident in saying that I disagree with his assessment. It is true that hitting the flop shot takes a good amount of touch, but I believe that touch can be developed.

Not only does the flop shot require touch, but it requires an aggressive stroke, great balance, tremendous club head speed, and last but not least... guts. If you are not committed and confident in your ability to pull off the flop shot, then you have no business attempting it. There are too many serious negatives that can happen from a poorly executed, uncommitted flop shot so let's go through the fundamentals to see what makes this shot so special.

Flopper Grip

The grip for the flopper remains neutral. It is important for your hands to be able to move freely in the backswing but they need to be solid through the impact position. A neutral grip will allow just enough hinge and movement of the clubface while setting the club in position on the way back. Keeping your right hand in a weaker position will help to hold the clubface through impact allowing the loft of the club to propel the ball upward. It's a must that you grip the club lightly during this shot to allow for maximum touch throughout.

Posture & Stance

The stance needs to be extra wide and open during the flopper. The extra wide stance allows for the needed stability throughout the shot. The flop shot is almost completely executed with the shoulders, arms, and hands. Opening the stance will allow you to swing freely across the body and allow for a full follow through. Your posture should match the posture of your full swing set up. Your bend should be at the hips with the knees flexed slightly and the back set at an angle, yet straight.

The Flopper has its own set up

Ball Position

Position the ball off the left heel as this will allow the club face to stay open past the impact position, which will give you maximum loft on the shot.

THE SHORT AND LONG OF IT

The flopper is a short shot that requires a long, aggressive swing. On the backswing pick the club up in a "V" shape by cupping the left wrist. This motion will open the clubface farther than the set up starts you, which will allow you maximum loft through impact. The length of the swing needs to be long in order to create the necessary speed to propel the ball the correct distance you are trying to hit it. The follow through should be equally as long as the backswing indicating the acceleration and speed that just happened through the impact position.

Aim to hit the shot off the toe of the club with your highest lofted wedge. This will still allow for the same high trajectory but it will also deaden the shot, which will give you the ability to swing as aggressive as you need to without the feeling of catching a "flyer" and sending the ball sailing over the green. When you strike the shot successfully off the toe you can always depend on the ball stopping very close to where it lands.

The biggest factor in successfully hitting the flop shot is judging when you can, and when you can't, hit the shot. The most important variable to consider is your lie. Without a decent lie where you can slide the club under the ball without the bounce on the club skipping up into the side of the ball then you shouldn't even consider hitting the shot. And never hit a flopper off a hardpan lie or when the ball is sitting down in thick rough. Make sure there is a sufficient cushion under the ball so the club can slide under it through impact or else the results can cost you multiple strokes.

The Best Flopper Game

Growing up on the Kansas plains, I found there were plenty of obstacles to practice flopping balls over: Flopper over the barn, flopper over the Cottonwood tree, flopper over the grain silo, flopper over the tractor, flopper over the cow...get the idea? Grab a friend and a 60-degree wedge. Go out on the course or in a field and challenge each other to a shot making flopper contest. You know, like that commercial with Larry Bird and Michael Jordan playing horse...off the building, through the window, over the bleachers and nothing but net.

CHAPTER SUMMARY:
ESSENTIALS FOR PLAYING SCRATCH GOLF
THE SHORT GAME

➤The definition of the chip shot is; a shot that spends more time on the ground than in the air.

➤The definition of the pitch shot is; a shot that spends more time in the air than on the ground

➤The fundamentals and basic technique of the chip shot are the backbone of every short game shot around the green. Master the fundamentals, set up, and techniques of the basic chip shot and you will be on your way to a better all-around short game

➤Lean toward your target to promote a downward blow and to stabilize your movement in both chips and pitches. This helps to take away unnecessary movement in the technique.

➤Pick a spot where you want the ball to land and visualize how you are going to get your ball to that spot. Use your imagination!

➤Have a tempo to your short game shots. Find a way to swing the club back and through with rhythmic pace… tick-tock, one-two, or "Tiger-Woods" are common timing schemes people use to improve tempo.

➤Eliminate tension from your hands, wrists, arms, and shoulders. The more comfortable you are, the more likely you will be to hit the shot you need to hit

➤Hit down on the ball. The stroke can and may be short, but shouldn't "stab" at the ball. A descending blow is critical to consistent contact.

➤Less lofted clubs will help keep the ball lower and allow more "run" while more loft will help the ball into the air and produce less roll; technique stays the same.

➤When in deep rough a more lofted club will help the ball come out with more consistency. A steeper angle of attack is required for the results you are looking for.

➤A partial wedge shot is a miniature version of the golf swing. The in-between manner of this shot makes the timing and tempo of this shot one of the toughest to control.

➤The chest and shoulders lead the partial wedge shot away from the ball while the hips stay relatively quiet; the hips lead the downswing while the chest and shoulders follow.

➤Finish the partial wedge with a controlled and abbreviated finish.

JUNIOR GOLFERS ESSENTIALS:

➤Play games to help fuel your fire and keep your interest level in practicing the short game shots. Friendly competition with fellow juniors is a great way to begin developing touch and feel.

➤Find ways to challenge yourself to better your short game. Keep track of progress and reward yourself when reaching a goal.

➤Technique is not as important as developing touch and feel and learning how to practice the short game shots.

TOURNAMENT PLAYERS ESSENTIALS:

➤Technique is critical to your success under pressure. If you aren't confident that your technique will hold up under the pressure of competition then you need to find a professional to help you revise your technique until it is ready for prime time.

➤In a competitive setting it becomes more critical to pick the most specific target possible to land your ball.

➤Routine is a must in all short game shots during competition. Your routine needs to be your crutch under pressure. Be sure to have a rehearsed, solid routine for every short game shot.

➤Your imagination and ability to "see the shot" before you hit it is one of the best assets you can develop for tournament play. Practice this while you are practicing all short game shots.

➤Have a never-fail process for great tempo. In competition you will need to have ultimate control of your tempo and pace when it comes to the chip shots. Work hard on this in your daily practice.

THE SHORT GAME… The Great Equalizer

➤The Short Game is not age or gender bias. Techniques remain the same from one to another and can be equally developed by all golfers.

➤Kids typically have the physical means to practice the short game for hours as it can be physically grueling on the lower back to put the time in to have a great short game. Adults often have the mental capacity to focus on the task at hand longer than juniors making these the most noticeable differences.

➤Most Short Game Shots take little strength or athletic ability to become very good at them. Practice and good technique make you better. Period. No matter who you are.

CHAPTER

4

The Full Swing

"*My swing is so bad, I look like a caveman killing his lunch*"

— *Lee Trevino*

BUILD A SWING YOU BELIEVE IN!

Having worked hard at the pre-swing fundamentals, you now have a good base for which to build a golf swing around. By positioning your body in the proper way, athletically and strong, we can move the golf club on the proper path, along the correct plane with the best chance to return it to the ball with ultimate power and control. Without the basic, pre-swing fundamentals to fall back on, everything that we do while swinging the club becomes an opportunity for a bad habit to creep in.

I was on the back of the driving range one day giving a lesson when I got a call on my radio for information to who was on the practice tee. Being on the back tee of the driving range, put me a good 260 yards away from the other side of the range. I could see four people hitting balls and standing around on the practice tee. I responded to the inquiry by giving the names of who exactly was hitting on the other side of the range.

I apologized to the player I was coaching for the radio noise but the player said, "Never mind the interruption, how can you tell who is on the other side of the range? That has to be almost three hundred yards away and no one's eyes are that good."

"You're right," I responded. "I can't see their faces but knowing all the players that practice here, I can tell who they are by the way they swing."

The conversation went on for a few minutes and the player was extremely curious how I could tell who someone was JUST by the way they swing a golf club. As I started the lesson again, a group came up to the tee box near the front of the range. The player immediately stopped what we were working on and anxiously asked, "Ok, who is on the tee right now teeing off?" I obliged to his questioning when I realized what he was doing. The first man hit and I immediately said his name. The second gentleman played and before the ball hit the fairway I called out his name. On the third person teeing off I immediately recognized who it was by the way he took the club back. When the fourth player hit I had to watch the entire swing, the ball landed and I watched him walk back to his cart. The player quickly said, "So, I guess you can't tell everyone by their swing." As the group proceeded down the fairway and closer to us I soon could see that I didn't recognize the face of the fourth person in the group. I learned later that it had been a guest out to play that day, someone who was visiting for the first time.

The point of this story is that each individual golfer has their own personal, authentic golf swing. We are all built differently and we all have great variations of athletic talent. No matter if you are a tournament level golfer or a true beginner, you are always in the process of shaping your swing. Let me say that again as this may be the most important thing to know about the swing. YOU ARE ALWAYS IN THE PROCESS OF SHAPING YOUR SWING.

Visual learning is the best way to help train your golf swing. In this day and age of technology it is simple to find video on the Internet of just about every tour player's swing. The thing to remember when searching for a video of a player to emulate is to choose a player who is as close to the same body type as you. These days, many of us would choose to swing the golf club the same way that Tiger Woods swings it. But unless you are 6'2", approximately 200 pounds with less than 3% body fat and don't forget about the 28" waist, then he likely isn't the ideal choice. Instead, choose someone who is about your same height, weight and who has the similar body characteristics as you do. Look for arm length, leg length, and the length of torso relative to the rest of the body. There are numerous shapes and sizes on both the PGA tour and the LPGA Tour for you to choose from. If you don't have access to the Internet or if using modern technology scares you, then try to pick someone whom you know you will see on television fairly often.

When watching take note of the fundamental swing mechanics of your player of choice and begin to shape your swing to match. You will quickly notice that most players do many things quite different but the results are all similar, and often successful. The golf swing does have a textbook way of doing it, but the reality of it is that each individual has his or her own authentic golf swing. Think of your golf swing as your signature. Can anyone else really duplicate your signature? This is true with the golf swing, no matter who you are.

Many players feel like they need to change their swing in order for it to hold up under pressure situations. But what are the basic techniques and mechanics needed to have a fundamentally solid swing? Keep in mind while you are reading that you still will have your own style and your own authenticity in your swing. Fundamentals are important and critical to a good swing so that you can have TRUST every time your out on the course. It is your ability to trust your swing and accept what it gives you that will determine how your swing will hold up under pressure and over time.

Your golf swing is an ever-changing work in progress and you must constantly monitor your swing for potential bad habits that creep in as well as for subtle changes that you need to make to play winning golf. As you strive to play scratch golf you will see your swing go through many plateaus of performance. At times your swing may feel great and easy to trust while other times you will struggle and your swing might feel like an unfolded lawn chair. But it's how you react to each scenario and everything in between that will make you a championship player.

FULL SWING FUNDAMENTALS

Follow the same basic fundamentals of grip, stance, posture, ball position & alignment as you do for putting and all short game shots. Let's review the fundamentals as they apply to the full swing.

Grip
The most important part of the grip is that the handle of the club lies in your fingers and not in the palm of your hands. Having the grip in your fingers allows you to release the club using your hands in conjunction with the rest of your body. Using a overlapping grip, interlocking grip, or a ten-finger grip as discussed earlier is up to you. Most players tend

to use the overlapping or interlocking grip stating greater control as the main reason for their choice. But really there is no right or wrong grip when it comes to these three. I will say though, most of the golfers that I know that use the ten-finger or baseball grip, are all Red Sox's fans who still dream of one day taking batting practice in the shadow of *The Green Monster*.

With your hands on a club, position the "V's" that are formed naturally between your index finger and your thumb on each hand parallel and pointing in the same direction. You would like to have the "V's" pointing somewhere between the right ear and the outside of the right shoulder depending on how strong or weak you choose your grip to be. When you look down at your top hand you should be able to see at least one of your knuckles and possibly two also depending on how strong of a grip you want to have. Your thumb and index finger should also stay connected as much as possible on your both hands. This will help with the overall control of the club throughout the swing.

Your grip pressure needs to be comfortably firm, not choking, on the club. Place your hands on the club in a way so that you don't feel tension or tightness but be able to hold the club firm enough to handle swing speeds of more than 100mph. You'll also need to be able to release the club with great precision in a split-second when you are making contact with the ball, so again, you mustn't be holding it too tight. On a grip pressure scale from 1 to 10, a 7 would be perfect pressure.

Posture & Stance

Your stance for the full swing should be a distance that maximizes both balance and power in your golf swing. The insteps of your feet should be approximately shoulder width apart for most all shots but as discussed in the short game, the shorter clubs, such as your wedges will need a narrower stance. Use a wider stance for the longer clubs like the fairway woods and driver. Your stance should permit you to make a full swing while remaining in perfect balance and at the same time allow you to maintain your ability to turn the hips and shoulders fully.

The posture should go with the stance and allow you to be athletic and strong while making the necessary movements to swing the club. The secret to good posture is matching the lower body to the torso so that the two can work together in the golf swing and react to each other when needed. Remember that the major bend or tilt in your posture happens from the hips and not from the back. Create this bend by feeling like you are sticking your rear-end out away from you. This will in turn force your torso forward creating an angle in your back that will cause your center of gravity to point to the ball. You will now have that feeling of standing on the edge of a cliff and trying to peek over the edge.

Your knees must have enough bend in them so that you feel balanced and ready. Spread the weight in the lower body out evenly from heel to toe so that the upper body feels like it is ready to rotate freely throughout the swing. Too much bend in the knees is bad as it limits your ability to turn your shoulders in conjunction with the hips and too little knee bend gives you poor balance throughout the swing, which will force you to swing with less power.

One of the most common mistakes for amateurs is not maintaining the same distance from the ball on every shot. Standing too close or too far from the ball will force you to make to many manipulations in your swing. When you are too close you are in what is known as a "locked" position, which can cause too much of a lifting movement in the swing. Standing too far from the ball forces you to reach for the ball and will give you the tendency to lift and change your spine angle throughout the swing. Always remain the same distance from the ball no matter what club you are using.

Ball Position

Ball position and alignment can be one of the most frustrating deterrents in your golf swing and if you don't constantly monitor it then you will spray balls everywhere. You don't want to ever have the feeling that you are reaching to hit the ball. Having the correct ball position and alignment will not only encourage all the right movements in your golf swing but it will also give you more consistency in both your chosen ball flight and placement. The length in the longer clubs like the driver and your fairway woods will demand that the ball is placed further from you than other clubs but you still never want to have that feeling that you are reaching for the ball. The hands need to stay the same distance from the body on all clubs to maintain that consistency in the swing.

3 RULES OF BALL POSITION

1. Never put the ball behind your stance.

2. The wedges and short irons should never be further than center at address.

3. The longer the clubs should be further forward in your stance.

Alignment

Alignment is all about perception verses reality. You should never set up to hit a shot unless you feel that you are lined up exactly where you want to hit the ball. Any doubt in your alignment and you should immediately back off and start your routine over. If you are lined up twenty yards to the right or left of your target at address then your perception of what is reality is way off. This misperception is bad because eventually you will use your athletic ability and hand-eye coordination to change your swing to find a way to keep hitting it at your target. If this progresses long enough you will end up with a bad habit or swing flaw that keeps you from trusting your swing under pressure. If you have a coach or someone you trust with your golf swing make sure you have them check up on your alignment frequently. When that person isn't around then use the clubs in your bag as alignment tools by putting a club down on the ground that points in the direction of your target. Then use your eyes to check whether your feet, shoulders, and hips are set up parallel to the club on the ground. Use a second club placed parallel to the first one and on the outside of the ball to keep your clubface lined up properly. This should get any misperception in your alignment back to reality. Whenever you find yourself struggling with your swing and you can't figure out what it is that you are doing wrong, always check your alignment first.

A FOUR-PART SWING

1. Initial Take-Away

It is critical that you get the club started back correctly and on-line. The first 18 inches to three feet of your backswing is the roadmap of where your swing is going to go from this point. Many golf professionals will argue that the initial take-away is the most important part of the golf swing. I agree but also will tell you that the impact position is equally important.

The chest, arms, and club all move away from the ball together

It's very important that you set the club in motion and not the body. The reason you have worked so hard to set up to the ball correctly is so that your body can move the club on the proper path and plane throughout the entire swing.

The club head should start back down your target line and extend on that line for at least the first eight inches of your takeaway. Midway through your backswing the club should be positioned parallel with your stance line. Your hands, arms, shoulders, and chest should be working together freely to get the club to this position. From this point you are at a great spot to move the club to the top of the swing and into a perfect position.

The club is parallel to the target line during the backswing

The left arm should be fully extended and straight, almost in a reaching motion at the midway point of your swing. At address you want the arms, shoulders, and hands to form a triangle. For the first 12 to 18 inches of the backswing this triangle should remain in position indicating a smooth takeaway in which the shoulders, chest, arms, and hands worked together to start the swing. Most mistakes made here will cause even more problems throughout the swing so it's vital you get off to a good start.

The shoulders and arms form a triangle that stays connected initially during the takeaway

One big mistake to avoid is allowing the club to stray inside the intended path you want it to swing. If the shaft of the club is pointing to the right half way through the backswing you will be forced to make adjustments for the remainder of the swing in order to get back to the ball. These adjustments are inefficient movements that cause lack of consistency and reduce your power.

2. Getting to the Top of the Swing

From the midway point of the swing, let your hands and shoulders move in unison to propel the club into what is known as the "slot" at the top of your backswing. Although your hands and shoulders are working together they both have the two different motions to perform that make up the golf swing. The shoulders continue turning until the left shoulder has completely turned under the chin. It is much easier to make this move if you keep your chin a consistent distance from your chest throughout the swing. It is the job of both the shoulders and the arms to transport the club to the position at the top of the swing.

The club should be on plane at the top of the swing

The left arm should be fully extended

The torso should be coiled with the back pointing towards the target

The Full Swing

The right arm can be a telling piece at various points throughout the backswing. The right arm should stay in front of your torso at all points throughout the backswing with the right elbow pointing straight to the ground at the top of the backswing. The right elbow forms a 90-degree angle at the top of the swing forming a perfect platform for the hands to brace the club.

The right arm aids in the extension away from the ball

The right arm begins to fold to support the top position

The right elbow should be pointing at the ground at the top of the backswing

Full extension is key to a solid and powerful swing

Hinging the wrists is a major source of power and consistency

Getting the center of gravity behind the ball is key to great shots

Backswing Checkpoints / Lower Body

There are a few checkpoints for the lower body that you must ensure in order to achieve a great position at the top of your backswing. The lower body needs to show three things:

1. Your weight should have gathered on the instep of your right foot.

2. The left foot should stay flat on the ground in order to help restrict the turning of your hips.

3. Your right knee should stay flexed consistent to where it was at the address position.

Backswing Checkpoints / Upper Body

1. See if your left shoulder has made its way under your chin. The chin should be far enough away from your chest so that the shoulder doesn't need to "knock" the chin out of the way.

2. The clubface should be square at the top, parallel to the plane of the left arm.

3. The right arm should be pointing to the ground and away from the side slightly.

The Full Swing

It is important to create and maintain width on the backswing. Width is the relationship of the hands to the rest of the body throughout the entire swing. If the hands are too close to the body at any point during the backswing you will end up having to compensate for this later in the swing. The wider you can make your backswing the more time you will give yourself to create power and speed in your swing. Your shoulders and arms are equally responsible for creating the proper amount of width. If proper width is created the triangle is created that aids in keeping the club square and on line throughout the swing. If you get either elbow out of position it can cause a lot of headaches in the rest of the swing and makes it difficult to return the club to the ball.

If you allow your right elbow to get too disconnected from your body it is what we call a flying elbow and this means your arms are out of sync with what the rest of your body is doing.

You also want to avoid getting your right elbow too connected to the body on the backswing. If your right elbow is too connected it will shorten your swing taking away power and control. This also makes it difficult to coordinate your downswing because of the tension it adds to the swing.

Pic 1—The elbows should be close together at the top of the backswing indicating control and power in the swing

Pic 2—A laid-off position can cause a variety of bad shots

Pic 3—The flying elbow keeps you guessing which way the ball is going

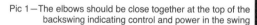

3. The Transition

At some point, your swing needs to stop going away from the ball and begin returning to the ball. There needs to be a split-second in time where that transition point pauses or is still. A common thought for this position is, finish your backswing. What this simply means is that you need to make sure you have completed the backswing before you begin the downswing.

There is no doubt that the faster the club is moving at impact, the further the ball will travel. It seems like a simple concept however achieving the maximum power and speed is easier said than done. Most amateur players want to rush the downswing, letting all that coiled energy go at the first moment possible is a daunting thought but it is also one of the most dangerous and harmful ideas in a golf swing. Letting out all the power you have created from the backswing needs to be done properly in order to get the most out of your swing. Rushing the downswing only takes your body out of sequence, changes the timing and takes away any possibility of lagging the club. Rushing causes the shoulders to outrace the arms, the arms to outrace the hands, and the hands to outrace the club in the downswing. The energy and speed of the club is expended much too early and as a result the club head is actually losing speed as it approaches the ball which is precisely the point in which the club head needs to be moving the fastest in order to generate maximum power.

Take your time at the top of the swing. You've worked hard to get to the top properly so enjoy the position that you have successfully moved your arms, shoulders, hands, and club to before starting the downswing. Make that transition point a smooth and soft transfer. One of the best swing thoughts here is to feel the pause as you start your transfer from the top of your swing to downswing. Shift your weight from your right side to the left side and at the same time let the arms begin to fall from their current position. If done smoothly you will feel a slight bull whipping action with the club.

In the following picture, notice that the arms are the first part to start moving. By giving the arms a head start on the shoulders and chest it helps keep the shoulders from racing ahead of the arms and allows the shoulders and arms to work together to create a powerful approach to the golf ball.

The arms "fall" toward the ball as the weight transfers to the left side

4. On the Way Down

On the way down you are generating increasing power and speed from the time you start your downswing all the way through impact. It is important to keep the body and the club in the right positions while trying to achieve this difficult task. Although you are swinging with all your might it is critical to keep this power under control.

One of the most important aspects of the downswing is maintaining your extension and at the same time preparing to release the angle that you created with the sharp hinging motion on the backswing. Feeling the sensation of keeping your arms and hands the same distance from your chin on the way down will help to keep your swing on plane. The other important factor to consider at this point is that you must eliminate any unnecessary lateral movement. Allowing your center of gravity to move too far forward on the downswing will change the timing of impact. Unless you make the same lateral motion identically the same on every swing your timing, power, and accuracy will be complicated. It is imperative that you keep your center of gravity behind the ball until you have reached the impact position.

Reach Back Low, then Go!

Start the club on-line as you begin the backswing making sure that you are not too far inside. The club head should start back down your target line extended for at least the first eight inches of your takeaway. Now here's the secret: Keep the club head as low to the ground as you can during this initial takeaway. By keeping the club head low to the ground, you will find that you will stay online much easier and more often, the triangle formed by the arms will be maintained throughout the take-away and make it much easier to get square at the impact position. So what's the swing thought to make this all happen? Reach Back Low, then Go!

TOP 5 DRILLS TO POLISH YOUR SWING

1.SHAFTS THAT PERFECT YOUR BACKSWING— Find yourself three old shafts without the club heads. Use one of the shafts as your alignment line. Stick the first shaft in the ground matcing your shaft plane line at set up. Push the shaft in the ground until it sticks out about 2 ½ feet. Place the second shaft should be four inches behind the first shaft and two feet beyond, away from the body and sticking straight in the ground.

Once the shafts are in place take three practice backswings for each ball you hit. Watch the club head as it ascends up the plane line. Notice how your hands hinge as you work the club up the swing plane and how your arms extend fully to avoid hitting either obstacle. Enough practice with these shafts will help build you a backswing that won't fail.

2. VARY YOUR DISTANCES— Start with your 9 iron. Make a full swing, but only hit it 50 yards. Be sure not to shorten the swing but control the speed of a full swing to control the distance. Hit the next one 80 yards using the same control but with a little more speed. The next one, hit 100 yards. Then 120 yards which will amount to around a 75% swing. (depending on your level of play and strength factor) Now hit your nine iron using 90% speed and then finish with an all-out, full speed 9 iron. In all, you are going to hit the same club using seven different speeds and the ball will travel 7 different distances. Take notice which speed produces the most consistent results. Do this drill with all of your clubs including your driver and you will start to realize how many different shots you can produce.

3. PERFECT YOUR TURN— To realize how important rotation in your swing is place a towel on the ground, grab your 7 iron, and tee a ball up high on a tee. Kneel down on the towel and extend your arms so the club head is set up exactly at the ball.

The knees drill set up position.

In this drill you are isolating a feeling in the swing, the feeling of turning your shoulders and torso. You will also get a feel for how the arms are required to extend in order to make solid contact. When you get good at your 7 iron, try your 5 iron then your driver. Keep in mind a drill is used to build confidence and gain sensation in certain parts of your swing. Your main goal in this drill is not necessarily to produce great shots, but more to learn the feeling of a good turn, one of the two major motions in the golf swing.

4.CLOSE YOUR EYES AND TRUST— When you face a shot you have to hit you must be able to trust your swing. One of the best drills I know to trust your swing is to hit balls with your eyes closed. Set up to the ball as you normally do prior to the shot. At the last second just before you pull the trigger, close your eyes. Hitting shots with your eyes closed will allow you to have a better sense of what your body does during the swing. Ultimately you will still have your target in mind, but the senses really take over and allow you to feel your swing. When you start hitting solid shots you will gain confidence that you can trust your swing.

5.MIRROR A FLAW SET UP— The set up is critical to swinging the club consistently and with power. To perfect your set up practice setting up in front of a full length mirror. Use the mirror to check your posture, your ball position, your weight distribution, and whether or not your arms are hanging properly in relation to your upper body. You can immediately see if you need to pay special attention to your posture or how you are distributing your weight. If you understand how you need to set up you will soon see if you are setting up in a way that will allow you to swing to win. You should do weekly check-ups in the mirror to monitor your set up.

CHAPTER SUMMARY:
∘ESSENTIALS FOR PLAYING SCRATCH GOLF
THE FULL SWING

➤The full swing is a product of your fundamentals and can only be as good as your fundamentals. Once you have your fundamentals set you can build your swing around them.

➤Everyone has their own individual swing. No golf swing is exactly the same so find what is yours and learn to love it.

➤You are always shaping your swing and you will be for the rest of your golfing life.

➤Find a player of similar build, preferably on the professional ranks, and watch that players swing. Visually you often can pick up tips on how to improve your own swing.

➤Constantly monitor your swing for potential bad habits and for subtle changes that may need to be made to play winning golf.

➤The first 18 inches of the backswing set the road map for where the rest of the swing is going to go. This is one of the most critical points in the golf swing.

➤Set the club in motion, not the body. The body's job is to support the motion of the club.

➤Midway through the backswing the club should be set parallel to the target line with the toe of the club pointing to the sky. This gives you the best chance to arrive at a great top-of-the-backswing position.

➤The swing is a perfect combination of the body rotating, the arms lifting, and the hands hinging all in sequence and with great timing.

➤Your weight should gather over your right side during the backswing and gently shift throughout the downswing to the left side. This weight shift conducts the consistency in which shots are hit.

➤At some point the swing needs to stop the club from going away from the ball and start to return it back towards the ball. This transition point needs to be smooth and flawless to produce winning shots.

➤Don't rush the downswing but let the club fall towards the ball. The un-coiling and release of the hinged wrists will allow for a consistent, powerful impact position.

JUNIOR GOLFERS ESSENTIALS:

➢Juniors, start shaping your own individual swing from a very young age.

➢Give yourself an equal amount of time to work on your fundamentals as well as the shape of your swing.

➢Managing the amount of lifting, turning, and hinging as you develop your own swing is important.

➢Swing hard, as hard as you can. It is much easier to teach a softer swing than a harder swing.

TOURNAMENT PLAYERS ESSENTIALS:

➢The swing is what holds up or fails under pressure, so build one that you can rely on and trust.

➢It is just as important for you to understand your golf swing as it is for your fundamentals and techniques to be sound.

➢When you play in tournaments don't put the pressure on your swing, allow your swing to be the weapon it should be. Trust it.

THE FULL SWING— The Great Equalizer

➢Men and women, young and old, everyone has the chance to develop a good, fundamental golf swing. Certain techniques are going to come easier for some but all have the chance to conquer the game.

➢A solid golf swing takes hard work, dedication, and the understanding that the golf swing is a never-ending work in progress. The individuals who grasp this are the ones who have the chance to become Scratch Golfers.

CHAPTER

5

Sand Play

> *"The difference between a sand trap and water hazard is the difference between a car crash and an airplane crash. You have a chance of recovering from a car crash"*
> — *Bobby Jones*

THE SAND

One of the most intimidating aspects of golf is the sand and the intimidation starts the moment you hear the name, sand trap or pot bunker. These two names alone infer that sand is a trap that it is there with sole purpose to capture your ball and ruin your score for that day. You hear golfers talk about the sand on the course like it is a horror movie: "The pot bunker on hole 11 is as deep as an African tiger pit," or " The sand was as soft as quicksand, I went in to find my ball and found two golfers from the day before, instead." Yes, the sand can be quite frightening but as the above quote by Bobby Jones suggest, there is always a chance for recovery.

The truth of the matter is that sand bunkers are simply positioned on the course by the designer as an obstacle for the players to attempt to avoid, which is all part of what makes golf such a fun challenge. Think about it, nothing feels better than hitting the perfect shot onto a heavily bunkered green or into the middle of sand-laced fairway. Your confidence goes up and your game gets charged. It would be pretty boring to play a course with no sand, no water, no trees and no trouble, wouldn't it? Bunkers are merely obstacles, deterrents, and somewhere you would like to avoid on the course but they are not impossible to play out of, unlike the water where you have no choice but to take your penalty shot.

I was in the fairway of the second hole of a US Open qualifying tournament in South Florida. I was standing over a relatively simple 8-iron shot off a flat lie with virtually no wind. My yardage gave me the green light to go flag-hunting because it allowed me to use a comfortable swing, not forcing me to doubt at all what shot I was about to hit. I went through my usual pre-shot routine and then pulled the trigger. I struck the ball perfectly! The ball took off like a bullet right at the flagstick and then sailed like a kite quite a ways past it. It ended up directly behind the hole, behind the green and in one of the greenside bunkers. As I looked in disbelief from the fairway I turned to my caddie and said, "That was the longest eight iron I think I have ever hit." I was in complete disbelief that I had mis-hit the shot so far over the target. Distance control has always been a strong point in my game and to this day I still can't explain how or why that ball traveled to that back bunker.

As I approached the green, I lump formed in my throat as I got close enough to look at the shot that I was now facing. My ball was sitting in the dreaded, fried egg lie, on the downhill slope of the bunker, facing a green that severely sloped away from the shot. Looming on the other side of the green and directly behind the hole was another bunker that was twice as deep as the one I was currently in and the total distance between the two bunkers was only about twenty paces. The USGA had positioned the hole location in the narrowest part of the green in an effort to insure the hole was difficult enough for a US Open.

I had made a good solid par on the first hole and was on my way to feeling confident and strong about my game. I had played this course before in US Open qualifying and I knew that it would take two or three under par to have a chance at advancing into the sectional qualifying. I had survived the first hole jitters and had made two good swings to this point on the second hole. I was beginning to get that upset feeling over the seemingly bad break but then quickly reminded myself that I had hit the shot exactly as I had wanted so I accepted responsibility and prepared to hit the next best shot I possibly could.

I stood on the fringe just below where my ball lay in the bunker surveying the shot ahead of me. My initial thought was to hit the ball out sideways to the left just so I could assure my next shot would be on the green. It was a tough decision because the buried lie wouldn't allow me to put any spin on the shot and the slope of the green, speed of the green, and the lack of green to work with made it appear that the ball had a better chance at ending up in the bunker on the other side of the green. The problem with hitting it out sideways was that I would almost certainly be left with at least a forty foot putt that was mainly downhill and virtually impossible to stop closer than 10 feet from the hole. Being this was the US Open, I decided to hit the shot at the hole. My first goal was to make sure the ball got out of the bunker. The last thing I wanted was to have the ball right back in the bunker with a similar shot staring me in the face. I picked a landing spot on the fringe hoping that the longer grass might slow up the ball enough to keep it on the green and give me an attempt at a par putt.

I widened my stance and dug my feet in a little. I leaned with the slope of the hill and opened the face of the club as much as I could. I took the club almost straight up in the air and dropped it abruptly just behind the ball. The ball popped up into the air and landed softly on the fringe exactly where I had picked out for it to land. It hopped forward onto the green and then began racing down the hill. The ball just slid past the edge of the cup, probably taking a minute to peek into the hole on the way by, and then rolled off the green and into the other sand bunker on the opposite side of the green.

I couldn't have hit that sand shot any better than I did. Under the circumstances and with the lie and amount of green I had to work with, Tiger Woods might have been able to stop only one out of twenty on the green from where I was. Ok maybe two. The point is, I couldn't be disappointed or upset, I simply had to move on to the next shot.

When I walked over to the opposite bunker I first noticed that I had a perfect lie sitting just on the upslope of the bank heading up to the flagstick. I had about 10 feet of green to work with between the bunker and the hole, which wasn't bad, but when I got to my ball in the bunker I realized I could not see the green and just barely see the top of the flag. I dug my feet in with a wide stance, opened the face of the club, leaned my shoulders with the slope of the hill and swung with perfect tempo. The club slid beautifully under the ball and I watched as it floated softly up into the air towards the flag. My playing partners yelled out something just seconds later the only of which I remember hearing, "nice shot!" I had holed out the second bunker shot and saved my par.

I went on to shoot two-under par that day and missed making it to the sectional qualifier by just one shot. But that bunker shot had boosted me with a shot of confidence during my round that kept me playing hard throughout the day!

How To Execute the Standard Bunker Shot

So how do you make bunker shots something that you won't dread and maybe are even willing to accept? Understand first that the playability of sand is significantly determined by the sand's particle size. In other words, not all sand is created equal. Geographic location, most often, is the main reason for a golf course choosing the type of sand it will use for its bunkers. Sand particle size and moisture content in the bunker will produce a variety of lies for your ball based on these factors: velocity, incoming trajectory and angle of ball entry. For example if you hit a low trajectory shot with high velocity into a bunker it will most likely bury in the sand. If you hit a high shot that enters the bunker at a perpendicular angle then you will most likely get what is known as the "fried egg" lie, which is a lie where your ball penetrates the sand leaving a ring of sand around it. Understanding the type of sand you are playing out of can make all the difference in the type of shot you are trying to execute.

Like many other short game scoring shots, you must have a positive and aggressive attitude to be successful. If you step into a bunker afraid, or not believing that you are going to hit a good shot then the chances have just increased that you will hit a poor shot. You must approach bunker shots with the attitude that you are in a potential scoring position if you hit a great shot. This attitude will allow you to be calm, relaxed, and most importantly aggressive with the shot.

SAND SHOT FUNDAMENTALS

The setup you use in your bunker shot will dictate the type of swing you can take and how the club will behave once it enters the sand. Like all your shots, it is important to master the fundamentals of: grip, stance, alignment, ball position, as perfect technique is what leads to perfect execution.

Grip

Weaken your grip for the bunker shot. Take your same grip that you use for the full swing but move your left thumb on top of the club at 12 o'clock. The right hand will then follow the direction of the left hand and turn counter clockwise and the right thumb will also be close to the top of the handle. This weakened grip will reduce the rotation of the clubface at impact. The less rotation in this shot, the better your results will be.

Chapter 5

Stance

Your stance should be wide, very wide. You want to be as wide as you can get and still be fairly comfortable. The width in the stance eliminates some of the unwanted lateral movement and helps to stabilize the lower body. Your feet, hips, and shoulders need to all be aligned, and slightly to the left of the target in an open position.

Clubface & Alignment

Open the clubface to be pointed slightly to the right of the target. Relative to the alignment of your feet, hips, and shoulders, the clubface should be about half of that to the right of the target. This open clubface increases the loft on the club, which allows you to use the design characteristics of the sand wedge, particularly the bounce on the sole of the club. An open clubface also allows you to hit the sand shots high and soft which is most often the desired shot out of sand.

Ball Position

Ball position for a standard bunker shot should be towards the front of your stance or just opposite the left heel. This ball position promotes a higher trajectory and also encourages the club head to slide through the sand easily.

Perfect set up for the standard sand shot

THE SAND WEDGE CLUB

The sand shot is different than any other shot you will hit on the golf course. Most of the movements and techniques contradict everything that the full swing requires and demands in order to hit consistent shots, which is the main reason for amateur golfers struggles in the sand. The sand shots that are most often hit are those using your sand wedge club.

The sand wedge club, like the shot itself, is built differently than the rest of the clubs in your bag. Its attributes are well suited for the sand but also work well all around the green. If you want to drop your high handicap or take your low handicap and become scratch then the sand wedge must become one of your best scoring weapons in your bag. The sand wedge is usually the shortest, most lofted and also the heaviest club in your bag. That combination makes it much easier to propel the club head through the sand far enough to get under the ball. Standard pitching wedges have around 48 degrees of loft but the sand wedge can have anywhere from 52 degrees of loft up to more than 60 degrees. When you get stuck in a greenside bunker with a pin cut close to the edge of the green, the more loft you have to work with, the better. Grab your 60-degree!

Understanding how the sand wedge works will help you to execute it properly. The flange that runs along the sole of the club head extends lower than the leading edge. This causes the club to act like a rudder when it strikes the sand. It skids through the sand easily instead of penetrating too deep and causing a flub. The flange is also wider from back to front than the soles of your other irons are, which is another reason the club glides through the sand instead of digging deep.

So as you can see, the main objective of the sand wedge club is to keep from digging too far under the ball. Every design aspect in the club has a feature that helps prevent this action from happening therefore you must also have the motion that keeps you from digging the club into the ground.

HOW TO MAKE IT LOOK EASY

The standard bunker shot is all about technique and not about strength. The effort applied shouldn't be any more than what you would use for a thirty-yard pitch shot from a perfect lie in the fairway. Shorten the swing for bunkers as you don't need or want a long flowing swing with a lot of body motion. Keep your grip pressure light throughout the swing and maintain an easy rhythm and tempo while you swing your hands back to about shoulder height. The club head speed that is generated in this shot comes mainly from the arms and hands. Break your hands early in the swing and then cock them all the way. This shot is very much controlled by the hands and arms and very little is done with the hips and legs. Notice the cock in the wrist in this picture sequence.

Pic 1-2-3—Sand shot sequence.
The backswing, impact position and follow through

When you hit your sand shots properly you should notice that there is a good amount of sand being displaced through the impact zone. There should be a good amount of sand being thrown forward toward your target. If you ever wonder how much sand you need to take in a basic greenside bunker shot, try this test: Get in the bunker and set your ball into a perfect lie somewhere flat. Bring with you a bottle of sand off your golf cart or some sort of bucket that you can fill with sand. Hit bunker shots until you hit one that comes out high and soft the way you want to hit them. Look at the divot you took for that perfect shot and then take the bucket or bottle of sand and see how much sand it takes to fill the hole until it is exactly the way it was before you hit the shot. You'll be amazed at just how much sand you took to hit the shot and I bet its more sand than you thought you should take.

The sand that you are taking to hit the shot should be thrown forward, towards the target and at a fairly low trajectory. These are the key factors that indicate whether or not you have slid the club properly under the ball at the proper speed. When you consider the amount of sand that you are displacing versus the distance the ball is traveling, you will start to realize the importance of producing the correct amount of energy at impact. That energy is called club head speed and club head speed is the most important characteristic needed in the sand shot.

If you swing the club towards the ball slowly with very little aggression then your chances of chunking the shot and leaving it in the bunker increases greatly. The other common mistake that you can't afford during a round if you ever want to score low, is the dreaded skull shot. This is most commonly the product of decelerating into the impact zone, which then causes your body to feel like it needs to lift or help the ball out of the bunker. Ladies this is your most common mistake. To fix it, remember, down means up in golf. In order to get the ball up in the air you must hit down on it! In bunkers when hitting down, you have to trust that the design of the club will get you through the soft sand, the technique you have worked hard on perfecting will keep you from digging, and the speed of the club head at impact is going to propel the ball softly up onto the green.

Most amateurs have only one greenside sand shot that they use for every occurrence in the sand. The problem with that, is that sometimes the hole is right next to the bunker, which requires a soft shot that stops quickly and other times the hole is on the other side of the green, which requires a shot that lands, and rolls. With only one type of sand shot you are not able to go after the flagsticks, which means you will always have a lengthy putt to complete your up and down and get your sandy. There are several sand shots that you must learn if want to attack the flagsticks all of which require that you become skilled at taking more or less sand with the shot. For most high handicappers, knowing how much sand to take to control the distance of their bunker shot is the biggest problem. When you want the ball to come out of the sand, land on the green and then roll a good distance, you need to hit quite a bit further behind the ball. If you want the ball to come out of the sand and then stop immediately, you need to hit much closer to the ball, maybe as close as one inch behind it or more. Very rarely will you ever want to pick the ball cleanly out of a greenside bunker without taking any sand at all. This is one of the most dangerous shots in golf and a shot that can quickly get away from you.

The three lines in the sand represent different impact zones for your club to control the distance of your shot.

SPEED IS KEY

If you only remember one thing from this chapter make it be that when it comes to bunker play, speed is key. You always need to be accelerating when you approach impact with the sand. When you are in a pressure bunker situation, which for high handicap players can simply mean just being in a bunker and for competitive players could mean when the tournament is on the line, the best thing for you to remember is to accelerate into the shot. If you want to be consistent from the sand you must be able to insure that your club head is gaining speed when it enters the sand. Your technique will take care of the rest of the shot as long as you take care of moving that club with good speed through the sand.

BURIED LIES

Don't get discouraged when you walk into a bunker and see that your lie is buried or sitting like a fried egg. This shot can really get into your head if you allow it. I know it is hard to be happy about seeing a buried lie in the bunker such as the one I had in the US Open Qualifying but it really is rare that you end up with such a bad lie and stance that there is nothing you can do with it. Buried lies in reasonable spots really aren't that difficult if you understand what it takes to get them out.

First lower your expectations for this shot. This is where you need play the percentages and the percentages say that you are not going to hit the buried lie bunker shots as close to the hole as you do the perfect lie bunker shots. Simply because of the fact that you can't get enough club on the ball at impact, which means you will lose some control.

Hitting the ball out of a buried lie requires you to force the club to penetrate deeper than normal into the sand. You want to take a divot that is so deep that it would take twice as much sand from your previously discussed divot test to refill it! Aim for a spot about two inches behind the ball with a shut clubface instead of open. The standard bunker shot requires that you line up slightly to the left and on a buried lie bunker shot you need to line up even further left. Lining up further left will accentuate the out to in swing that produces a steeper swing plane and the deeper penetration into the sand you are looking for. Lean your weight to the left until you feel like your right shoulder is slightly higher than your left shoulder, which again will help you to swing into the ball at a steeper angle. Position your hands ahead of the ball as it's your hands that will be controlling the technique of this swing.

This is not the time to try and dink the shot just over the edge of the bunker. No, this shot requires an all out effort by you while still maintaining control of course. Pick the club up with the hands by cocking immediately; forcing the club straight up, the arms will follow the lifting process as needed. Punch down at that spot two inches behind the ball that you have picked out at address, with a tremendous amount of speed. Keep in mind you are hitting down at the sand and not "through" the sand like you do in the basic bunker shot. There will be very little, if any, follow through on this shot. The sand will stop the club less than a foot after impact. The ball will pop out of the sand like a knuckle ball in baseball, with absolutely no spin and very little control. If possible you will need to allow for the ball to run when it lands due to this lack of spin.

THE LONG BUNKER SHOT

There is no doubt that one of the toughest shots to play consistently well in golf is the twenty to forty-yard bunker shot. This range is still within the range that requires an explosion shot but is just out of the range to hit a fairway bunker shot. The technique of this shot is quite effective but there is no doubt that even with proper technique you are going to need to get out and practice these shots and experiment with different clubs and the effort that you will need to put into each shot from the different distances.

For a twenty-yard bunker shot you want to experiment with your sand wedge all the way down to your eight iron to see what works best for you depending on the different lengths and lies that you will face for this shot. I like the 9-iron most of the time because it moves the sand much better than a wedge. You will find that certain lies will be more effectively hit with a less lofted club and better lies will allow you to use more lofted clubs. Keep in mind the difficulty level of the long bunker shot when it comes to your expectations of your outcome. Just as the buried lie won't allow you to consistently hit it as close to the hole as a standard bunker shot, the long bunker shot will only allow for you to get yourself in a position to use the rest of your short game to get the ball in the hole.

Sand Play

The setup for the long bunker shot is again a modification of the standard bunker shot. Because you will be using more of your body as well as your hands, arms, and shoulders in this shot you will only need to line up slightly left of your target. Remember that opening your clubface increases the loft so judge carefully just how high you want to hit this shot before you select the club you are going to use. In general, because of the difficulty level of this shot, you should reduce the amount of variables you change such as clubface angle. Set the clubface squarely to the target line and aim approximately one inch behind the ball. If you hit too far behind the ball you will come up short of the green, too little sand and you will fly one into the abyss beyond the green, so its imperative that you make a backswing that allows for control to impact without losing speed. You must create as much speed with this shot as you can. Keep your stance narrower than a greenside bunker shot and your head still. Swing with great rhythm and tempo and finish like you would finish a full shot from the fairway. The full finish will insure that you have accelerated through the ball and created the speed necessary to get the ball to the green.

There are different ways for you to control the distances on this long bunker shot. Already discussed is the use of different clubs beginning with your sand wedge and going down to as low as your 8-iron. By changing clubs you are really just changing the amount of loft for each shot. If this is the way you are currently controlling your distances try this approach. Change the loft of only one club by opening or closing the clubface. For example if you choose to use your pitching wedge on your long bunker shots and you end up on the outskirts of your explosion distance then "hood down" or close the clubface of your pitching wedge to take loft off the club to make up for the extra distance you need. You could also vary the distance behind the ball in which you hit the sand and still use your pitching wedge. This requires great exactness and probably the least calculating under pressure. The simplest and most effective way to regulate the distances using just one club is by adjusting the length of your follow through. The longer the shot the more you need to try to achieve a full, complete follow through. Like with any shot out of the sand, you must always be increasing your club head speed as you approach impact. There is absolutely no place in any sand shot for deceleration. As we stated before, if there is one thing to remember when its time to pull off the most meaningful bunker shot of your life, it's: speed is the key.

SHORT-SIDED

As you become a better player, you're undoubtedly going to start firing at more and more pins many of which are going to be close to the edges of the green. Along these edges of the greens waiting your arrival are shot stealing sand bunkers that come in all shapes and sizes. Avoiding the bunkers is of course your first priority but occasionally you are going to miscue and find yourself stuck on the beach. Getting up and down from these short-side sand bunkers is a must if you are ever going to play scratch golf and with very little green to work with this can be a very scary shot. Since I spent the entire first half of my golfing life in every front right bunker of every course due to a weak slice, I can tell you that this shot is manageable if you follow this easy to remember routine.

Set up as you normally would for a regular bunker shot but then move the ball slightly forward and open your stance and clubface a little more than usual. Now swing down and slightly outside-to-inside making sure you accelerate as you hit the sand behind the ball first. Make sure your aim is just to the left of your target because when the ball pops up and lands on the green it will have a little side spin on the ball, which will make it jump to the right. (Speed in the hands is the biggest key to getting the ball to pop straight up.)

TOP 5 SAND DRILLS

1. DRAW THE LINE— Find a flat, well-groomed area in the sand and draw a straight line 10 feet long. Take practice swings at the line trying to get the club head to enter the sand exactly on the line. If the first mark the club makes is two inches short of the line, chances are you would have hit that shot fat. Conversely, if you hit past the line you may be hitting rockets across the green.

2. SLIDE UNDER— Are you having trouble getting the feeling of sliding the club head under the ball? Find a 2 x 4 or a small piece of plywood and bury it about ½ inch below the sand on a flat lie. Put the ball on the piece of plywood and hit some shots really concentrating on hitting down on the ball. Keep in mind the proper technique to "hit down on the ball" is to cock your wrists to lift the club.

3. 10 IN-A-ROW— Expectations out of the sand are often out of place. This drill will help you to have realistic expectations and it will also

give you some extra practice in the sand. Find a standard bunker shot on a flat lie and take ten balls hitting to a green or an area as big as a small green. Hit all ten balls, in a row, out of the bunker. Once you have accomplished this, and only when you have hit all ten in a row out, hit ten in a row out that stay on the green. Next, hit ten in a row within 15 feet of the hole, then 10 feet, then 5 feet. You can see that you can do this for awhile, so make sure you set your goals for the practice session before you start. When you feel like you are getting good, practice from tricky lies and stances until you feel like you can hit every shot.

4. BASKET PRACTICE— Find a practice bunker with ten or fifteen yards of green to work with. Put a basket or a towel on the opposite side of the green to use as your target. Hit your first shot out of the bunker high and soft trying to fly the ball to the target. The next shot hit out low and have it roll the majority of the way to the target. The next one hit with some spin to see how much it rolls after it lands and which way it spins. Don't ever hit the same shot two times in a row.

5. STEP ON IT— Throw 15 balls into a bunker. Walk into the bunker but before you hit each ball, step on it first. That's right; bury the lie before you hit it out of the bunker. Tough lies will never seem as tough after hitting these buried lies. Repeat until you become skilled at getting at least 50 percent successfully out of the bunker.

CHAPTER SUMMARY:
ESSENTIALS FOR PLAYING SCRATCH GOLF
CH5 — SAND PLAY

➤Learn to accept that bunkers are a part of the game, don't fear bunkers.

➤You must have a positive and aggressive attitude towards greenside bunker shots, there isn't a delicate way to get a ball out of the sand.

➤Weaken your grip allowing the right hand to be the dominant hand in the swing and keeping the hands from rotating the club through impact.

➤Take a very wide stance to eliminate any unwanted lateral movement through the swing and to help stabilize the lower body.

➤Open the clubface to increase the loft and let the club do what it was designed to do, slide through the sand!

➤Position the ball slightly forward of the center of your stance.

➤Shorten your swing, cock your wrists, and use the right hand to dominate the downswing and create the necessary speed.

➤Keep the face of the club pointing upward through impact. The feeling should be a similar feeling to that of throwing a Frisbee.

➤Finish with your hands high, near your left ear. This helps insure that you accelerated at the ball and created the necessary speed to get the ball out of the sand.

JUNIOR GOLFERS ESSENTIALS:

➤Get in the sand on the practice range often and make the goal to hit the sand behind the ball.

➤Always swing will great acceleration on every sand shot. Out of the sand is the only place you should worry about when judging results.

➤Learn to finish with the hands high above the left ear and you will have a good sand game for life.

TOURNAMENT PLAYERS ESSENTIALS:

➤Sand needs to be a staple in your game. When you find yourself in the sand you should be thinking about making the shot.

➤Quality practice in the sand is a must. The more quality time you spend, the better bunker player you will be.

➤Practice out of all types of lies. Never let a bad lie get you down during a tournament. Be prepared for any lie or situation the sand offers you.

➤Remember, sand is considered a hazard. Your expectations should be that of a challenge any time you hit a shot in a bunker.

SAND PLAY- The Great Equalizer

➤Any player who has the guts to take a full force swing at the ball can be a good bunker player… regardless of your age, gender, or skill level.

➤Good bunker players have taken the time to learn proper technique, practiced diligently to become a good bunker player and maintained a positive and aggressive attitude towards sand

CHAPTER

6

The Mental Game

"*A lot of guys who say they have never choked have never been in the position to do so*"

— *Tom Watson*

YOU, AND YOU ONLY!

To truly develop strong mental skills I believe you have to spend some time alone inside yourself. Why? For the simple reason that there won't be anyone else on the course with you to help you when you're facing fast breaking putts, thick Bermuda rough or penalty laden golf holes. No, the only one on the course who can help you get through the all the tough golf shots and pressure situations is you, and the inner you. What's the inner you?

Haven you ever been on a tough course and just before hitting a difficult shot you hear a little voice inside your head? You know, that little voice inside your head that you are constantly in dialog with during your round. That voice that sometimes helps you believe that you can do it but also at times tries to get you to give in and not believe. That voice you are hearing is your inner you.

Still don't know what voice am I talking about? Think back to when you first learned to swim and how swimming the width of the pool was a challenge. When your swimming skills became good enough to swim the width of the pool the challenge then became the length of the pool. As you sat there looking to the other end of the pool that voice inside you may have said, "Go for it! You can swim far now." If you believed in yourself then there was probably not much more dialog and off you went. But if you didn't believe you were ready for such a task then you may have talked yourself out of the challenge and waited until another day. That inner dialog between you and the inner you, is all part of your mental game at work. Still not sure what I'm talking about?

How about when you first were learning to ride a bike? Probably every time you crashed your mother or father or whom ever was teaching you, picked you up off the ground and told you to get back on the bike and try again. But before you got back on that bike seat I bet your inner voice had something to say about it. If you did get back on the bike then your inner voice was positive and encouraging and even if you crashed again you took one step forward towards developing your mental toughness. But if you gave up and put the bike away for another day, then your inner voice must have been negative and your mental development was slowed.

Your goal as a golfer is to develop a positive inner voice and shut out all the negative self-doubt that continually tries to creep in. Easier said then done, sure, but know this: those players who mope around the golf course constantly belittling themselves, blaming their equipment or believing they are victims of bad luck, are the easiest ones to defeat, if your in a match play tournament, and the ones who won't be there in the end, if your playing a stroke play tournament. Why? Because they haven't developed a confident positive mental approach to their game. They let everyone and everything negative around them get inside their head and interfere with that inner voice dialog, which then influences them in a negative way.

If you are a tournament golfer, you just can't afford to have any self-doubt about your game at all. If you truly don't believe that you can compete against anyone in the field or if you are intimidated by the course then you won't compete and the course will eat you alive. But if you do believe in yourself and in your game and your attitude about the course you're playing is a positive one then you definitely have a chance. What it comes down to is this: if you want to become a golf champion, it's what's inside you that matters the most!

Like I said before, if you want to develop a strong mental game then you need to spend some time alone inside yourself. Here are some ways you can work on your mental game skills to help you play mentally tough golf.

TOP 5 MENTAL GAME DRILLS

1.RANGE SCORECARD GAME— Go to the range to work on your game. Don't take a friend, a coach or a family member with you, just you a basket of range balls and an old scorecard from one of your favorite courses. Play out the golf holes on the scorecard using the yardage on the card and the flags or targets on the range to determine whether or not each shot is successful. Hit the shots like you would on the course, driver first then as many irons, hybrids or fairway woods it would take to get you on the green. Go through the entire scorecard adding pressure to certain holes by pretending you are hitting over water or there is out-of-bounds lurking on one or both sides. Now don't let yourself off the hook by giving yourself credit on a shot that you don't pure or flies the opposite way you pre-determined in your head. Play the entire scorecard before you leave the range. Don't forget to go through your pre-shot routine before every shot just like you would on the golf course. Before playing the qualifying for the 2006 Honda Classic I spent two weeks after my practice rounds on the range going through the scorecard. Consequently I knew what club I was going to use for each shot of every hole. It was a great feeling of confidence!

2.VISUALIZATION— This is an increasingly popular technique practiced by many top athletes of sports. This again involves the need for you to be alone by yourself, preferably in a relaxing atmosphere or environment. Imagine yourself performing certain parts of your golf game in a positive way. For example suppose your putter has been unreliable lately and you just can't seem to lag any long putts close. Try fixing the problem mentally by imagining yourself putting repeatedly perfect lag putts from 40,50 and 60 feet in length. See yourself two putting from above the hole on super fast greens or rolling in breaking putts from every angle. It's OK to imagine the most difficult putts going in as you want to keep all your thoughts and imageries positive.

Try visualization five to ten minutes everyday and always just before you hit your drives. If you have been having trouble keeping your drives in the fairways, then imagine yourself hitting your drivers so that they always land exactly in the middle. Don't forget to visualize the path the ball will take through the air to land in the middle. Do this just before you tee it up and I think you'll notice a positive increase in your performance.

3. HOCUS FOCUS— If your concentration or focus is weak during your rounds, try this technique. Before your next tee shot, stare at your golf ball for five minutes just before stepping on the tee. Notice the dimples,

the color, the number and the lettering on the ball. Now when you tee up your ball, focus on the letters while noticing the color and dimples on the ball as it sits on the tee. In other words, focus solely and only on the ball. See how long you can go before your concentration is broken and you begin looking or thinking of something else. Were you able to concentrate until you hit the ball? During your next round see if you can block out everything and focus solely on the ball.

4. DEVELOP WINNING ROUTINES— The scratch golfer knows that playing great golf is not an accident; it is a series of well-executed actions performed within a game plan. Next time you find yourself hitting great shots on the course take the time to notice exactly what you are doing. How are you stepping up to the ball, how many times are you waggling the club before hitting, what is your mind thinking of just before taking the club back and how much time are you taking to hit each shot? You will probably find that your well-executed actions are routines that keep repeating. That's a good thing! Now after that round go write down exactly what routine you were doing that produced such great shots and putts and practice repeating them. Always note what you were thinking of or focusing on during those days of great shot making or great play. Maybe you weren't thinking at all? Also note what you did just before you arrived at the course, what you ate and any other factors that you can remember that may have aided you in your superior performance. Soon you will have your own written guide to follow on how to play great golf every time you go to the course.

5. DUMP THE GARBAGE— Tournament golf is all about staying mentally positive. No matter what negative things are going on in and around you, you still have to be able to stay positive mentally if you want to win. Now every golfer experiences negative thoughts and feelings at some time during a round whether on a missed fairway, missed green or a missed putt. The key is to try to get rid of those negative thoughts and feelings that arise throughout a round as soon as possible. To do that practice this technique: Every time you go to the back of your golf cart or return to your golf bag imagine you are dumping out all the negative thoughts, anxiousness, stress, self abuse, hopelessness, frustration, nervousness and anything else that might be disrupting your play. Don't pull out a club or dare approach your ball until your mind is clear. What's more important than hitting your next shot is that you take the time to get rid of any negative garbage that has crept into your confidence, which could easily manifest itself into bogeys and other high numbers.

Next time you are on the course and you have just played a poor shot try taking a walk to the edge of the fairway and dump the negative garbage in the rough before returning to your cart or golf bag to play your next shot. You'll soon begin to stop those multiple shot miscues and become a much tougher shot-to-shot player.

CONFIDENCE: *My First Win*

It was a noticeably cool September morning, as my father and I walked the short distance between the 15th green and the 16th tee box at Hidden Lakes Golf Course just outside of Wichita, Kansas. I pulled up the hood on my WSU sweatshirt to protect my ears from a fierce wind that had begun to blow out of the north while tried to add up my score in my head. Up to this point, I had never beaten my father on a single golf hole and being a former coach, he knew better then to let me win one either. Number 16 was a 157-yard par 3-hole over a lake with a bunker to the right of the green and trees off to the left. My father took out his 7-iron from his bag and hit a beautiful high cut that landed softly on the green about twenty feet from the flag. I was up next and being only 10 years old I needed a little more club then a 7-iron. I selected a 5-wood that I knew I could hit high in hopes that it would clear the lake and land softly on the green like my father's ball. The wind was really blowing now so I aimed extra left of the flag to play my usual slice shot, which I hoped might get helped by the increased wind. I pulled the club back, trying hard not to think about the lake or the bunkers and then let it rip. I watched in amazement as my ball went up to the left of the green and then began curving back towards the flag just as I had imagined it. The ball landed hard on the front left edge of the green and then proceeded to roll up passed my fathers ball and in to within two inches of the hole. I was about to throw up my arms and shout for joy when I felt my father's hand come to rest on my shoulder as he said, "Nice shot son. Now let's go up and make those birdie putts." I grabbed my putter out of my bag so fast that three other clubs came out with it and then ran all the way to the green to mark my ball. I anxiously stood and watched as my father's birdie putt just lipped out on the left side of the hole. I replaced my ball, took my stance and somehow knocked in my putt. My first birdie and my first win.

What you have to know is that losing is part of learning and what I learned was I hated it and that fueled my desire to get better. Winning, on the other hand, breeds confidence and when you are confident you will be mentally tough under pressure. Practice winning!

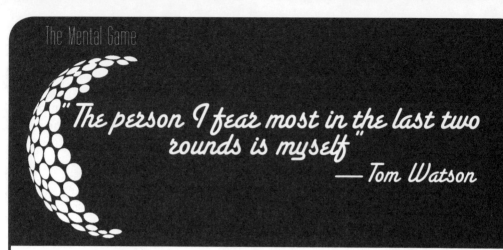

"The person I fear most in the last two rounds is myself"

— *Tom Watson*

CHOKING

Playing golf in what I like to call your "comfort zone" is something we all do but are not acutely aware of while it is happening. Your comfort zone is when you are playing golf status quo, or you are playing how you always play. The comfort zone is different for everyone. For a scratch golfer making a lot of pars, a few birdies, and some bogeys mixed in is a comfortable round. Your swing feels good and you seem to have good feel around the greens and you are playing, what you consider, a normal round of golf. For the high handicapper your comfort zone might be making double and triple bogeys while throwing in the occasional bogey. No matter what your playing level is, you have a comfort zone.

Now what about when you are playing out of your comfort zone and having a noticeably better day on the links than what you are used too? You're in unfamiliar territory and feeling very uncomfortable about it. This is when it can happen, this is when you can choke. You skull a bunker shot over the green into the water, you chunk a wedge from fifty yards, or you snap hook a driver out of bounds putting a quick end to your uncomfortable round of exceptional golf and putting you right back into your comfort zone.

For you scratch players this uncomfortable zone would be like those days when you start out hot and birdie three of the first four holes then make a few pars and realize while standing on the 8th tee that you are three under par. The fear of being out of your comfort zone makes you hit the next two balls out-of-bounds and you record a nine on the hole. Now you're right back in your comfort zone at two over par and wondering when your next birdie is going to come along.

For you higher handicap players, it might be coming to the 17th tee realizing that you have a chance to break 100 for the first time that has you feeling uncomfortable. If you can somehow play the last two holes in at four over par then you will set your all-time low round. Unfortunately it never happens. You inexplicably seem to find a way to get back into your comfort zone as quickly as possible and record a final score of 103.

If you've played enough golf then you know exactly what I am talking about. The question is, how do you keep it going when it's going good? The answer is, you have to be ready for it, by expecting it! You clearly can't force great golf to happen because if you could we would all be the best golfers in the world. What you can do though, is choose to be ready for it and accept it when it does happen. You need to plan, visualize and dream of playing great golf and be able to feel the sweaty palms and nervous butterflies while doing so. You need to put yourself into the situation as much as possible using your imagination when on the range and by actually doing it when on the golf course. When it happens you have to remind yourself that this is the reason you go to the range and beat balls and spend hours practicing all those putts and put the time, sweat, and heart into this game. If you are caught off guard when you play well your body and your mind will find a way to get you right back into your comfort zone before you even know it. You have to be willing and able to play outside of your comfort zone. If you are ready and willing to accept the nerves and feelings that come along with playing well, then your chances of continuing to play well increase tremendously.

Along with welcoming the feelings associated with playing great golf, you need to have your pre-shot routine to fall back on. A good pre-shot routine is not only a physical routine but it is a mental routine that you can lean on throughout a round of golf.

5 STEPS TO A GOOD ROUTINE
1. A mental trigger point or starting point
This can be as simple as when you pull the club from the bag or when you fasten the Velcro on your glove. This is not only the signal that your physical routine has begun, but it is also your cue that this golf shot you are about to hit is the most important thing in your life for the next thirty or forty seconds. The trigger point tells you its time to focus and concentrate on the task at hand.

2. Dial into the target

Take time to pick as specific of a target as you can. Don't just pick a tree, but a leaf on a certain branch of the tree. Don't aim at the building in the distance but pick which window you are going to aim at. Take time to concentrate on that target and how you intend to hit your ball there.

3. Get comfortable

Make sure you are physically and mentally comfortably with the shot. This is where your set up is so important. If you have spent the time to set up to the ball well you should have no trouble getting comfortable. Mentally you have to be confident you can pull the shot off exactly how you imagine it.

4. Commit to the shot

This is the point of no return. If there is any doubt you must discipline yourself to back away and start over with your routine. This commitment comes from everything you have done to this point. Only you really know if you are 100% committed to the shot... only you!

5. One Last Look

Take one last look at your target. When your eyes return to the ball let the shot begin and make it happen.

A good routine will act as your security blanket on the golf course no matter how you are playing but especially when you are playing better than normal. When you play out of your comfort zone, your mind is assaulted with thoughts that keep you from thinking about the task at hand, which is your next shot. You begin to think about your score, and what if I would have, and I can still birdie the next hole and so on. You have to focus your mind on the shot at hand and that's it.

Most of you will say that is easier said than done. But keep in mind you are the one making the decision about what you will think about out there on the course. We all have the choice of what to think about and when you are playing better golf than you are used to, you need to choose to think about your shot at hand. You need to trust that your pre-shot routine is second nature and if it's not your crutch to lean on under pressure then you know what to work on next time you are at the range!

SLUMPS

Self-confidence is much harder to build than it is to destroy as no one can stay focused, motivated or self-confident their whole life or every time out on the course. A simple three-putt on the first green or fat wedge from 75 yards, can crush a golfer's trust and confidence that may have taken weeks to build. But let's face it, there are going to be times when your performance is going to fade and if not rectified then you may even fall into the dreaded slump; losing confidence in yourself, your swing, ability or in your overall game. If that happens then it's important that you be honest with yourself so that you can diagnose the problem properly. Ask yourself the tough questions like: have I been putting enough time and effort into all areas of my game? Have I lost your self-discipline or determination on the practice range? Am I putting too much pressure on myself to perform above my abilities when on the course? Once you find the root of your performance problem, then you will need to be patient and take careful calculated steps to get yourself out of the slump. It can be a process that takes time so during this time I suggest you write down everything you go through, making sure to note if there was any one specific thing that may have been the key to getting you out of your slump. Maybe it was something positive your coach said, a new practice routine, a new swing thought or simply getting yourself in better shape. Whatever it was that got you out of your slump, writing it down will aid you later on if something like that happens again. If you can't figure out how to get out of your slump then it's time to go back to your fundamentals.

GO BACK TO THE FUNDAMENTALS

When things go wrong with your game and you can't figure it out, the basic fundamentals are where you will need to go back to when retooling. You've heard of the K.I.S.S. rule? Keep It Simple Stupid. It's been taught to all of us at some time in our life and still stands true today. While it's great to have a multitude of shots or creative ways to hit a golf ball, too many choices can sometimes cause confusion, which can then bring about frustration and get you away from your fundamental swing. When your game is on and your swing feels great, go right ahead and try new things, venture outside your comfort zone and experiment. That's how you get better; that's how you grow as a player. But when your game is off and giving you fits what do you do then?

Keep it simple stupid and go back to your fundamentals. Start over like you are a beginner taking your first lesson and re-teach yourself your grip, posture, stance, ball position and alignment. When you go back to the fundamentals, you'll be able to problem solve much better. You'll quickly find out which fundamentals were lacking or out of sync in your golf swing and then you can make the adjustments needed and get back to playing great golf.

This back to the fundamentals approach can be applied to all areas of your game as well as all areas of your life. As a student in mathematics, when I was stuck on a problem, I can't tell you how many times my teacher would prescribe that I go back to the root of the problem and start again. Going back never seemed right to me but in the end I was always able to work out the problem. In English class, when diagramming sentences, you are taught to find the fundamentals first: noun, verb and adjective. Without these fundamentals you can't figure out the more difficult parts of the sentence structure and you fail to dissect the problem. Having good fundamentals doesn't always garuntee a perfect swing or perfect play but it does help put the odds in your favor to have a good performance and to avoid that word that every golfer hates to hear, bogey.

THE FIRST TEE NERVES

We all know that there is nothing more intimidating then hitting off the first tee especially if there are two or three groups of players waiting in line right behind you to tee it up. But even more intimidating than that is hitting the tee shot on the first tee of any tournament, or in this case for me it was the Honda Classic Qualifier at The Fox Club in Port St Lucie, Florida.

Most great players of any sport will tell you that it is quite normal and healthy to have some butterflies right before a game. It helps to get the adrenaline rushing and to bring you into a conscious consciousness that you will need to be in to focus properly. The sweaty palms and the feeling that you're going to throw up will go away as soon as you hit your first good shot, then it's game on and time to go low. Unfortunately sometimes just the opposite can happen and that, I'm sorry to say, is where this story is heading.

I stepped onto the first tee box after hearing my name and city of origin announced by the PGA official and went through my normal preshot routine. I looked down the fairway to see where the trouble was located on this hole, which normally played as a par-5 hole, but had been adjusted to a par-4 for the tournament. There was a bunker in play on the right side and trees and water off to the left. When I miss a tee shot, I typically miss to the right so I thought I would aim down the left fairway just incase. What went through my mind next was totally out of character for me. I got a swing thought that repeated in my head, "Swing slow and easy." Totally the opposite of my normal rhythmic swing, "Swing slow and easy." I couldn't get it out of my head. I addressed the ball and slowly pulled my club back and then slowly began the downswing towards the ball. The only problem with the slow and easy swing was that on the way down I couldn't control the club head as normal and I came over the top and pull-hooked the ball through the trees on the left and down into the water. A disastrous start to the tournament and crushing blow to my confidence.

Amateur players take note, because this could be the best advice for you about first tee nerves. Take a few deep breaths. I don't mean just two or three, I mean like five or six. Concentrating on slow deep breathing reduces excess muscular tension especially in the shoulder and neck region and helps to clear your mind of unwanted thoughts. Ever watch an Olympic high jumper right before they attempt an extreme height? They take multiple deep breaths to relax and limber their upper body for the movement needs to get over the bar. How about a baseball pitcher right before he throws a fastball on a 3-2 count to a known home-run hitter? You will definitely see a few slow deep breaths there. Finally have you watched a tennis player right before serving against a break or set point? That's right, deep breathes.

Tension builds up in the muscles under pressure and you need to relieve that tension before you ever start your swing. If the tension is too great you will most likely become anxious and speed things up. This will change any rhythm that you may have gained on the range or been feeling in your round and send you into a hurry up and get it over with mode, which is how your mind tries to reduce the stress. This is when you need to be consciously competent of what is going on within you and slow down your behavior by taking a few deep breaths. Practice adding deep breathing to your pre-shot routine and see if you don't feel more relaxed and under control when the heat is on.

WHEN YOU GOTTA MAKE IT!
The Four-Foot Putt

The four-foot putt that you have to make can be the toughest mental challenge in golf. It seems that a shot that requires little or no athletic skill, zero strength, and such a short stroke shouldn't be that difficult to accomplish.

Consider the task and more importantly the situation in which you might need to make a four-foot putt. As an example lets say you have made two bogeys in a row early in the round and you now face a left-to-right downhill slider of four feet. You are trying to avoid a third bogey in a row and trying to keep from digging yourself a hole that is difficult to get out of. You need to make this putt! You need to salvage the beginning of your round that is slipping away and give yourself a reasonable shot at posting a low number. What do you do to make this putt? How do you insure that you will roll it with the proper line and pace and hear that clinking sound of the ball falling into the cup? How do you make it when you gotta make it? The answer is, quit trying and start playing.

Imagine a fifteen-foot long, six-inch wide board lying on the ground. If you are asked to walk across it, you would probably hop on it and scamper to the other side like it was nothing. Now, suspend that same board fifty-feet in the air and walk across it with no net and no safety measures attached. It now becomes a much different walk across that board because suddenly there are consequences to the slightest mis-step. If you think too much about what would happen if you were to step too far to the right or just a little off to the left, you might get tight and nervous and worrying too much at just how you are stepping. This consciousness of how you are trying to do, adds pressure to what you are trying to accomplish. The board being suspended high in the air is pressure enough and you don't want to add to that pressure if you can help it.

The same thought process accompanies the four-footer. The fact that you have already made two bogeys early in your round and are in danger of getting off to a horrible start is similar pressure to walking that board high in the air. The situation has created the pressure and so you don't need to add more pressure to what you are trying to accomplish. What you should do is approach the putt with the same attitude you would if that board were lying on the ground. Step up to it and stroke it like you know you are going to make it. Let yourself have an easy, free attitude and don't spend any extra time thinking about what you are doing. Remind yourself that you have made thousands of four-foot putts prior to this one so why not let this one be just another make.

This is again when a solid routine both mentally and physically can play a huge part in your success and failures on the golf course. If you allow yourself to stick to your routine and don't try to do anything out of the ordinary you will increase your chances of making the putt. You have worked on your routine doing the same thing over and over letting your mind focus on the same thing throughout, now is not the time to change what has worked so many times before. Trust your routine and hit the putt with the attitude that you know you are going to make it and that will give you the best chance when you gotta make it!

HOPE & FEAR
April 7th 1999

It was April 7th, 1999, I was on a weekend golfing trip with three of my friends in central Florida. Since it was coming up on Master's week we decided to get out of town and play what we call, A Major, to decipher who was currently the best golfer amongst us. A major for our group takes place every time there is a major golf event being held on TV and the only stipulation is that we must all travel at least an hour away from home to an unfamiliar course to equal the playing field. For this major the course selected was Royal Oak, a golf course in Titusville Florida owned by the Canadian PGA, which was a good three hours from where any of us lived.

We arrived early in the afternoon with plans to play a quick 18 holes of practice before sundown in preparation for the real game the following morning. After a speedy check-in and cart grab, we were on the first tee all ready to hit our drives in less than fifteen minutes of our arrival. We were well into our sixth hole when the dark clouds started rolling in for the usual Florida late afternoon showers. By the eighth hole it was raining and by the ninth it was pouring.

After trying to continue to play through the storm with no luck, we decided to finally head into the clubhouse and call it a day. We must have been the last ones in because when we arrived, the parking lot was empty and cart attendant was nowhere to be seen. We put are clubs under cover and headed to the bar. The scene there was more of the same with only one bartender and one older gentleman sitting by himself at a corner table drinking a Coke from a Styrofoam cup.

As we purchased a round of drinks and nachos, the traditional after golf order, the Canadian golfer in our group asked the bartender who the man in the corner was as he thought he recognized him. "That's Moe Norman," the bartender said.

"Moe Norman!" I said. "I want to talk with him do you think he'd mine?"

"I don't know let's ask him. Hey Moe these guys want to talk with you if it's alright," the bartender hollered over?

"Sure. Can't play golf. Can't play golf," Moe said eluding to the rain that was pouring down outside.

We went over and respectfully introduced ourselves, shaking his hand and asking to sit at his table. He didn't say yes he just kind of mumbled and gestured with his hand what looked like to us as, "have a seat." I had so many questions for this legend I didn't know where to begin. I asked him three questions and what I got from him has stuck with me and in my game to this very day. I'd read a lot of articles and books written and seen numerous interviews and videos about the man they called, 'the best striker of the golf ball to ever play the game' but the advice and wisdom that I got from Mr. Norman that day I have never seen in print, heard tell of or seen in any interview with anyone. It was like he was giving me something that he had never given to anyone else and I think it was so that I could give it to you and the golfing world here in this book. Think long and hard about the following interview and try to see if it makes as much sense to you as it did me and then put it into your game.

"So Mr. Norman, how often do you play golf now?"

"Oh I play everyday, play everyday!" he said with confidence and a smile and in a sing-song voice that always went to a higher pitch at the end of his sentences.

"You play everyday?" I asked again in disbelief.

"Sure do, sure do. Play everyday, yes everyday, right here in my mind." He said lifting a finger and tapping on his forehead.

Wow! I was blown away. All the stories of Moe Norman that I had heard and maybe hadn't really believed were rushing into my head and gaining credibility with every word he spoke.

"What do you think of today's game and all the new power players?" I asked.

"Walking tree stumps, they are. Walking tree stumps. Nicklaus is the only player to ever bring 15 clubs to the golf course. You know what the 15th club was? He asked pointing to his head. "His mind. Yep, only guy. The rest of 'em are all walking tree stumps."

"What about Tiger," I asked.

Moe didn't say anything. He just kind of sat there, stared straight ahead and then took a drink of his Coke. I wondered if he had heard me or if he just didn't have an opinion on the great Tiger Woods yet. I asked a different question in hopes of getting an answer to both questions.

"Do you like the way any of the new player's play?"

"Nicklaus is the only player to ever bring 15 clubs to the course. The rest of 'em all play with too much, hope and fear, hope and fear I tell ya," Moe said. "All these guys out there can shoot 70 to 75 everyday but none of 'em get any better because they all have too much hope and fear, hope and fear!

This time I was the one who sat there in silence and just stared straight ahead. I had just heard the most useful and insightful information ever about what it takes mentally to play tournament level scratch golf. Moe was so right on the money with what he had said. Think about it, how many times have you stepped up to hit a shot and said to yourself, I HOPE I pull this shot off or how often have you addressed your ball and felt FEAR about the shot you were about to hit. Hope & fear was exactly how I had been playing this game and I know it's how most amateurs play as well.

I'll never forget that conversation we had with Moe and the wisdom that he passed on to us, that rainy April day. For a guy who they say didn't like to talk to strangers, answer questions or make new friends, he sure took time with us to make us feel like he was just one of the guys and our friend for life. Moe Norman sadly died of heart failure in 2004.

Author with Moe Norman.

CHAPTER

Futuremetrics

"The will to win is important but the will to prepare is vital"

— *Joe Paterno*

ARE GOLFER'S ATHLETES?

It's an argument that I've heard and taken part in for many years. Growing up in a family of athletes I was always on the NO side of that argument that is until I started playing golf tournaments and really practicing to lower my handicap. What I've learned in those years and through film observation of today's tour players is: there are golfers who are athletes and the golf swing does require a great deal of athleticism. Strength, power, flexibility, balance, core stability, body awareness, even endurance are all physical traits that every golfer (yes even you weekend warriors) must possess, no matter what your handicap. If you really want to hit it CONSISTENTLY BIG then this is the most important chapter for you.

I believe that everyone has within their self a certain amount of natural talent for their chosen sport, some much more then others, and others much less than some. And that talent, once maximized, cannot and will not go any higher then what that person has within them. They will eventually reach their ceiling of natural talent, in other words. As a golfer you too will, at some point in your life, reach your natural talent ceiling of your ball striking and shot making skills. But does that mean once your ceiling is reached that you will never be able to go higher and improve your game? Not at all! Improving ones athletic ability is the answer to raising that ceiling. And since you can always improve in this area, then the sky is the limit as to how much better of a golfer you can become.

I play weekly with a group of guys that collectively all need to improve their athletic ability. They are all good strikers of the golf ball with good tactical minds but all lack the athleticism needed to consistently hit the ball long and straight. I believe this is mainly from their lack of flexibility and core-strength but also because of their non-sport-specific training programs that they are each doing off the golf course.

What I have found, after being the Ginny pig to every golf fitness/training program and every new training device know to man, is that a golfer needs: a training program that incorporates the skills of various other sports to help them improve their athletic fine motor skills, a flexibility workout routine which they can do before and after a round of golf, improved club head speed with the use of elastic bands and small weights and a core workout with the use of weighted balls that will increase lower body strength and improve dynamic balance. Since I have always been a subscriber to the theory that if you work hard at improving your athletic ability then you will in turn greatly improve whatever sport you are a participant in, I took up the task to put together a golf training program with the best of the best golfer-specific exercises that I call Futuremetrics.

What is Futuremetrics?

Futuremetrics is a training program designed to improve a golfer's core strength, flexibility, power and endurance, using the athletic skills of various other sports. Most golfer's I've met, want to improve their athleticism, but if it means running in circles for an hour around a track or on a treadmill or doing an uninteresting weight room workout most just don't have the time or the discipline to make it happen. But if the training program is as enjoyable to them as being on the golf course is, then a player will likely work much harder at improving his or her athleticism and reap the athletic benefits which will then show in his or her overall performance.

For you serious tournament players, think about this: conditioning can no longer be seen as an unnecessary add-on to your practice routine. Just as a committed amateur athlete spends time on their technique, so must you spend time on your fitness to be the very best you can be. But just going to the gym and working out is not the answer because pure strength may make you stronger, but it won't maximize your club head speed. In fact, training to increase your overall strength could actually make your swing slower and that's why you must make sure your training program is golf-specific.

THE SECRET TO HITTING LONGER DRIVES

What's the secret to longer drives? Well, quite simply it is a matter of club head speed and club head speed is ultimately determined by how quickly your muscles respond and contract. Pure strength may make you stronger, but it won't maximize your speed. You must put this formula to memory: Force = Mass (x) Acceleration. What that means is that the faster you can accelerate your golf swing, the more force that will be applied to the ball, and the farther it will travel. Futuremetrics has shown to increase club head speed by an average of 25 percent. While it could be argued that club head speed is only one small facet of a golfer's overall game, it is highly correlated with a player's handicap. In other words, the lower a player's handicap is, the higher their club head speed at impact tends to be. In fact, a 25 percent increase relates to a reduction of a minimum of 3-5 shots off a golfer's handicap. Do you think this is an important facet to becoming a scratch golfer? Absolutely!

ADDITIONAL ADVANTAGES OF A FITNESS TRAINING PROGRAM:

➤ More general physical endurance

➤ A stronger heart

➤ More red blood cells carrying oxygen to the tissue, which means a slower heart rate with more rest between beats. (A heart beating 80 beats per minute beats 115000 times a day; a heart beating 50 beats per minute only beats 72,000 times a day. A savings of 43,000 beats.)

➤ More muscle strength

➤ Better resistance to disease

➤ Decrease in body fat

➤ Lower blood pressure

➤ Increase of endorphins, which are natural brain stimulators

➤ Reduced stress and depression

➤ Increased self-esteem

THE STRETCH ROUTINE

It only takes about 10-15 minutes to stretch your primary muscles and increase flexibility, which can often be the most important factor in keeping you injury free. Flexibility helps to increase club speed, which results in power during your swing, and so increasing it should be a constant goal in your training. The pre-exercise stretch or the before the first tee stretch, I believe, should not be performed as deep as the post-exercise stretch. It is important to warm the muscles up before you play but not to over-stretch the muscles. With some players, stretching can help achieve a proper warm-up but in others it may actually increase their risk of injury and reduce their potential strength during physical exercise. There are many new studies in this area and all state that each player is different in the area of the pre-exercise stretch. You may want to experiment with deep and light stretching before each session. All studies do agree however, that in the post-exercise stretch, everyone is equal and should perform a thorough deep stretching routine to aid in muscle recovery, muscle soreness and injury prevention. Remember that any training program and stretching routine should be molded around your specific needs as a golfer. Try this stretch routine before the first tee.

➤ Start by rolling your neck around in each direction five times.
➤ Next reach both arms to the sky with your fingers laced together. Hold for a 15 second count. (Repeat 3 times) PHOTO
➤ Next, standing up, cross your left foot over your right and slowly bend down and touch the ground keeping your legs straight. Then switch your right foot over your left foot and do the same. (Repeat 3 times and hold all stretches for 10 seconds each time)PHOTO
➤ Next push up against a wall or golf cart at arms length with one foot slightly in front of the other. Keep the heel of the back foot on the ground as you lean forward straightening your back leg and stretching your calf muscle and Achilles tendon. Then switch legs. (Repeat 3 times)PHOTO
➤ Next spread your legs out wide to the sides and then lean to the left and right stretching the groin area. (Hold each side for 10 seconds before switching)PHOTO
➤ Next have a seat on the edge of the driver's side of the golf cart. Sitting up straight and using the steering wheel for leverage, bring the left hand to the right knee and put the right hand behind you and then twist. Hold for 5 seconds and then switch sides and twist. (Repeat 3

times each side.) PHOTO
➢ Next slide to the seat on the passenger side of the golf cart or sit on the ground to stretch your hamstrings and lower back muscles. With both feet extended in front of you, reach out and try to see how far you can reach past your toes. This is a good test of your flexibility. Top athletes of various sports can reach well past their toes. (Repeat 3 times or as needed)PHOTO
➢ Next stand and grab any of the vertical supports of the golf cart. Sit back into a chair like pose and hold for 8 seconds. (Stand and repeat 3 times.)PHOTO
➢ Next stand and pull one leg up behind you while holding onto the golf cart vertical support. (Hold for 8 seconds and switch legs)PHOTO
➢ Next stand up on one leg and put the foot of the other leg up on the golf cart. Now lean all your weight onto the elevated foot and then back off. (Hold for 8 seconds switch and repeat 3 times)PHOTO
➢ Finally grab a golf club and hold it above your head. Drop one hand off letting the club drop behind your back. Reach behind and pull down on the club(Hold for 8 seconds. Switch hands and repeat.)PHOTO
➢ Lightly jog in place for 30 seconds to 1 minute.
➢ Now you're ready!
➢ Continue to stretch during the round.
➢ Remember post-round stretching should be much deeper and include specific areas of muscle soreness, tightness or weakness.

l. Increase your overall range of motion.

2. Generate more club speed. which means more distance off the tee.

3. Increase your shoulder and hip turn in the loading of the backswing.

4. Increase consistency by maintaining good posture at address and throughout the swing.

5. Reduce the risk of injury.

OF DRILLS & POSES USED IN THE FUTUREMETRICS PROGRAM:

Knee to Chest Walk

Walk while pulling your knee up towards your chest as high as you can with each step.

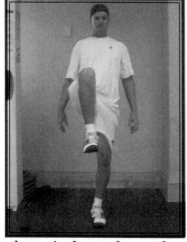

Swing to the Sky Twists

Kneel on a towel. Take a 10lbs. medicine ball in both hands and hold at arms length out in front of you. Then swing arms and ball behind you to the right side by turning your shoulders only until your chin is resting on your left shoulder. Then swing up to your left side all the way to head high until your chin is on your right shoulder. Then do opposite side.

Standing Two-arm full body Rotational Pulls

Attach your resistance band to the bottom of a door or golf cart. Reach down across your body to grab the band with both hands, turning your hips and shoulders towards the ground. Pull the band up towards your chest and then push it on up towards the sky. Lower back towards your chest and then to the ground. Repeat all reps then switch sides.

Weighted Ball Circles

Sit straight up on a mat with your legs flat out in front of you. Take your weighted ball in your hands and twist back to your right and set the ball down directly behind your back. Then twist to the left, reach behind yourself and pick it up. (Repeat this circular transfer of the weighted ball 50 times.)

Weighted Ball Wall—Throws

In an square stance, stand about 3 feet away from a wall. Facing the wall, hold the weighted ball with both hands. Load the legs and rotate your torso as you prepare to throw the ball. Explode with your legs and your core as you throw the ball into the wall. Catch the return of the ball and immediately load again and rotate for another throw. (2 sets of 15 throws from each side)

Forward— Step Lunges

Step forward into a lunge so that the back leg knee goes to the ground and the front leg knee doesn't go past the toes of your front foot. Keep your back straight!

Crossover— Step Lunge

Stand straight up holding a 10lb ball or weight at your chest. Step your right leg across your left leg as you go down into a lunge position. Be sure to try and keep your back straight and your shoulders facing forward as you perform the lunge. Stand back up straight and then crossover left to right. Repeat.

Chair Lunge Pose

Stand with your feet shoulders width apart and your arms hanging naturally by your side. (for extra resistance hold a golf club or a weighted club in both hands in front of you) Prepare to sit as if you are sitting in a chair. As you sit allow your arms to raise up until a perfect balance is maintained. Hold for 3 seconds and return to a standing straight position and repeat.

Popeye Forearm Super Strength Drill

Take a 5 lbs weight that is tied to a bar hanging 2ft down. With your palms facing down roll the weight up and then down three times. Next try it holding the bar with your palms facing up.

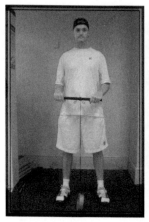  

Swing to the Sky Lunge

Stand in a lunge position with the back knee resting on the ground. Swing a 10lbs medicine ball from low to high turning only the shoulders on the way back and reaching high to the sky on the follow through.

The Superman / Golfer Pose

Lay face down on a mat extending your arms out over your head. Lift your arms and legs as if you were flying. Hold the pose for 10 seconds. Next try just left arm and right leg then right arm and left leg.

Full Standing One— Arm Pulls

Take a wide stance and place one end of your resistance band secure under your left foot. Lunge down and grab the other end of the band and pull it up across your body and above your head to a full right arm extension.

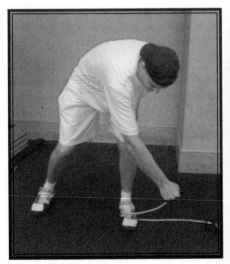 

Forward Lunge with Twist

Start in a standing position, hold a 5-10lbs medicine ball in front of your body. Step forward into a lunge. In the lunge position, rotate the body 90 degrees to the left while holding the medicine ball away from your body. Then rotate back to the front and step up to a standing position. Repeat this process alternating lunging with right and left legs.

The AB — Wheel Workout

Start on your knees with your hands positioned on an abdominal wheel of some kind. Roll out as far as you can and then using only your abdominal muscles, pull yourself back to the start position.
(10-100 Reps)

Super Low Back Extensions

On a mat, get on your hands and knees. Tighten your abdominal and lower back muscles by drawing your belly button in towards your spine. While keeping your back flat, lift your right arm and your left leg until they are parallel to the ground. Keep your head in line with your spine by looking down during the exercise. Return to the starting position and switch to left arm and right leg (2 sets of 15)

Crunches

Lay flat on your back with your hands locked behind your head. Crunch your knees up to meet your elbows and then back down again.

Three- Cone Touch Drill

Place three cones in front of you to form a shallow 'V'. Stand in the middle of the 'V' about 1-2 feet from the middle cone. Standing on one leg, squat down and touch the right cone with your right hand and then return to a standing position. Do the same one-legged squat to the middle and left cones. Try to keep your back as straight as possible. Repeat this process 3 times and then switch legs. Mix the hand/leg combinations to develop better balance and strength.

Core Rowing Pulls

Attach your resistance band to a fence or golf cart at waist level and start with your arm straight and tension felt in the band. Set your body in an athletic position and contract your core. Pull the band until your arm is near your side even with your chest. Return to the straight arm starting position keeping the movement controlled.

Ice Skate Lunge

Just like it sounds. When you're training at the beach, on a sand volleyball court or on a clay tennis court this is one of my favorite leg strengthening drills. Without picking up your feet slide them out ahead of you one by one as far as you can lunge as if you are ice skating.

4-WEEK FUTUREMETRICS PROGRAM

The following is a level 3 sample of a 4-week Futuremetrics program. It always begins and ends with a 10-15 minute stretching routine. The number of reps for each exercise and the amount of time you hold each pose should be based on your current fitness level. Always when doing a new fitness program of any kind you should start at a level 1 and work your way up in moderation.

IST WEEK FLEXIBILITY.STRENGTH & ENDURANCE

Goal—
To increase flexibility, build overall body strength, and increase endurance.

MONDAY, WEDNESDAY & FRIDAY
➢ 15-minute stretch routine
➢ 1 mile run or walk
➢ 25-yard knee to chest walk-5 times (continuous) then jog 5 times with walk back to start
➢ 10 yard lunges- 5 times with walk back to start after each (continuous)
➢ Swing to the Sky Twists- (3 sets of 10 each side)
➢ Swing to the Sky Lunge – (Right side 3 sets of 10, left side 3 sets of 10)
➢ Superman/golfer pose – (perform all three poses 3 times each) (hold pose for 10 seconds)
➢ Chest Rolls - Lay with your back down and raise your knees. Take the weighted ball and shift it over your chest from side to side, touching the ground on each side 20 times. (Repeat 3 times)
➢ 100 sit-ups in 4 sets of 25 on a mat or using a fitness ball.
➢ Popeye Forearm drill. Roll weight up and down 3 times.
➢ Weighted club swings 30 times (tempo swings only)
➢ Stretch routine again and cool down

TUESDAY & THURSDAY
➢ 15 minute stretch routine
➢ 1 mile run or walk
➢ 25-yard knee to chest walk-5 times (continuous)
➢ 15-yard lunges- 5 times with walk back to start after each (continuous)
➢ Weighted Ball Circles drill (Sitting down, do 50 to the left and 50 to the right)
➢ Chest Rolls – (3 sets of 25)
➢ The superman/golfer poses (All 3 poses 5 times)
➢ Chair Lunges (5 sets of 10)
➢ 50 Crunches on a mat (5 sets of 10)
➢ 50 push-ups in sets of 10 on a mat or using a fitness ball
➢ Weighted club swings 50 times (tempo swings only)
➢ Stretch routine and cool down

2ND WEEK FLEXIBILITY, CORE STRENGTH, UPPER BODY STRENGTH

Goal—
To increase flexibility, upper body and core strength & club head speed.

MONDAY WEDNESDAY & FRIDAY

- 15-minute stretch
- 2 minutes on the Jump rope or 1 minute on weighted jump rope
- Resistance Band Workout: (Hook a resistance band to a golf cart or door at drill height: shoulder, waist or ground)
  1. Left shoulder pulls (2 sets of 10)
  2. Right shoulder pulls (2 sets of 10)
  3. left forearm pulls (2 sets of 10)
  4. Right forearm pulls (2 sets of 10)
  5. Full left side one-arm standing pulls (2 sets of 10)
  6. Full right side one-arm standing pulls (2 sets of 10)
  7. Standing Two-Arm Rotational Pulls (10 each side)
- Popeye forearm drill (Roll up and down 3 times)
- Scorpion pose (3 times each side hold each for 8 seconds)
- 100 crunchers 4 sets of 25
- 50 push-ups in sets of 10 on a mat or using a fitness ball
- Weighted club swings 50 times(tempo swings)
- Stretch and cool down

TUESDAYS & THURSDAYS

- 15-minute stretch
- 2 minutes on Jump rope or 1 minute on weighted jump rope
- 100 sit ups and 50 push ups in sets of 25 and 10 alternating
- Swing to the Sky Twists (3 sets of 10 each side)
- Swing to the Sky Lunge (Right side 3 sets of 10, left side 3 sets of 10)
- Sitting Two-arm full body rotational pulls(25 each side)(see photo)
- The superman/golfer pose. (All 3 poses Repeat 5 times)
- Scorpion pose 3 times each side
- Weighted ball circles drill (Sitting down, do 50 to the left and 50 to the right)
- 50 Weighted club swings (tempo swings)
- Stretch and cool down

3RD WEEK LEG STRENGTH.
LOWER BODY STRENGTH & BALANCE

Goal—
To improve lower body strength, core strength & dynamic balance.

MONDAY, WEDNESDAY & FRIDAY
- 15-minute stretch
- 35 minutes on Bicycle (level medium)
- 15 minutes on treadmill walking
- Forward Lunge with Twist(25-yards while holding medicine ball)(3 times)
- Chair Lunges 2 sets of 25
- 50 crunches in sets of 25
- Super Low back Extensions (1 set of 15 each side)
- Popeye Forearm drill (Roll weight up and down 3 times)
- 50 weighted club swings
- Stretch and cool down

TUESDAY & THURSDAY
- 15-minute stretch
- 30 minutes on treadmill, jogging (level, med-high)
- 25-yard knee to chest walks 10 times (continuous)
- 30 crossover lunges both ways (3 sets of 10 holding 10lbs)
- The Three Cone Touch Drill (Do all leg/hand combinations R-R,R-L,L-L,L-R)
- 100 sit-ups with 30 push ups alternating in sets of 25 and 10
- Super Low Back extensions (2 sets of 15 each side)
- Scorpion Pose 3 times each side
- Stretch and cool down

4TH WEEK REFLEX POWER AND MORE CORE

Goal—
To increase explosive power, reflexes and core strength.

MONDAY, WEDNESDAY & FRIDAY

- 15-minute stretch
- 1-mile sprint/walk/ jog—(change pace every 220 yards)
- 5 minute rest/stretch
- Core Rowing Pulls (2 sets of 20 each arm)
- The AB-Wheel workout:(Level 1:10 times, Level 2: 20 times, Level 3: 30 times
  1. Roll straight out 10 times
  2. Roll at a 45 degree angle to the right 10 times
  3. Roll at a 45 degree angle to the left 10 times
(Repeat all 3 times)
- Weighted Ball Wall-Throws (5 sets of 10 each side)
- Chair Lunge (3 sets of 10)
- Weighted Club Swings 30 times
- Stretch and cool down

TUESDAY & THURSDAY

- 15-minute stretch
- 1-mile sprint/walk/jog—(change pace every 110 yards)
- 5 minute rest
- Resistance Band Workout: (Hook a resistance band to a golf cart or door at the desired drill height: shoulder, waist or ground)
  1. Left shoulder pulls (2 sets of 10)
  2. Right shoulder pulls (2 sets of 10)
  3. Left forearm pulls (2 sets of 10)
  4. Right forearm pulls (2 sets of 10)
  5. Full left side one-arm standing pulls (2 sets of 10)
  6. Full right side one-arm standing pulls (2 sets of 10)
  7. Standing Two-Arm Rotational Pulls (10 each side)
- 100 sit-ups & 40 push-ups in sets of 25 and 10 alternating with no rest.
- Popeye Forearm Drill (Roll weight up and down 3 times)
- Weighted Club Swings 50
- Stretch and cool down

FITNESS NOTE

Once you have completed a four-week program access your fitness level before starting the next four-week session. If your fitness level is in the above average range, increase each week by ten to twenty percent by either increasing the number of times you do each drill or by decreasing the amount of rest between rounds or sets. Also cut back to a three days a week maintenance program using Futuremetrics days Monday, Wednesday and Friday of each specific week as your guide. You should design your Futuremetrics program to fit your specific needs. For example, if your endurance level is high but you are still weak in flexibility or core-strength then put more focus into these areas until you have equaled your endurance level and vise-versa. Look to add new drills that have similar results, every four weeks to keep the training program fresh and fun. And the benefits of golf fitness training are not reserved for the young. Golfers aged 55-105 will also benefit from strength and flexibility training both in terms of general health parameters and their performance on the course.

OVER-TRAINING

As with any conditioning program don't forget to add in days of rest to avoid over-training. Intense training without proper rest can lead to injury and or illness. Here are some signs of over training that you should be aware of:

➲ Consistent muscle soreness—It is natural to be sore as you go through the first few weeks of any conditioning program, as you are building up muscle strength. But persistent muscle soreness is not good and should be treated as signal to back off or retool your program.
➲ Sleepless nights—If you're having trouble sleeping through the night then your muscles are over worked.
➲ Not hungry or see a dramatic weight loss.
➲ Mood swings—If you're more irritable anxious or unmotivated.
➲ Getting sick too often is a sign of possible over training.
➲ Dizzy spells or light headiness.

When you are showing signs of over training the answer is always rest. Take a few days off and rest. If you feel the need to workout try something different like swimming, surfing or bike riding. A few days away from intense training can do wonders for you both physically and mentally.

If you are an active tournament player, your conditioning program schedule should be scaled down to consider the on course grind of tournament weeks. A competitive golfer's Futuremetrics schedule would look something like this:

➲ Strength training of core and other key muscle groups, 3 times a week—during tournament weeks keep the intensity high but the number of reps low. When not a tournament week, go with low intensity and high reps.
➲ Endurance training 2 times a week—distant running 20-30 minutes or bike riding.
Flexibility Routine—a stretching routine should continue to be performed daily.

TOP 5 TRAINING TIPS

1. Push yourself hard everyday!

2. Never say, "I can't!"

3. Accept the challenge of new exercises or more repetitions.

4. Make consistency a habit.

5. Enjoy the self-confidence that comes with feeling stronger, fitter and more flexible.

CHAPTER

Winning Ways

"*I've always made a total effort, even when the odds seemed entirely against me. I never quit trying; I never felt that I didn't have a chance to win*"

— Arnold Palmer

Once your swing is grooved and the shots are going where you aim, it's up to the many layers of focused practices and the saved memories of well-executed shots to get you around the tough courses and through each tournament round. Your performance on the course now becomes the only measuring stick that you and everyone else will use to evaluate your success. All of your practice rounds, off-course training and range work that you've put into your swing and game must show through in each opportunity you have to perform. And that's exactly what each round of golf should be to you: an opportunity to show off your game through your performance. All your goals and dreams and how you have planned to reach those goals and dreams is on the line each and every time you step on the course for a tournament round. And whenever your putting it all on the line, there's one thing left you must overcome, one thing left to endure, one thing left trying to bring you down and that's pressure.

No player who plays tournament golf can say that they don't feel at least some amount of pressure somewhere during a round. It's a natural reaction that everyone has when they are put on the spot to perform. The tournament golfer knows that it will all come out either in their swing or score whether or not they have been truly working hard in their practices or just been going through the motions. The player who has just been going through the motions will undoubtedly feel more pressure on each shot because that player knows deep inside that he or she hasn't properly prepared. That player will only have the hope that his or her best performance will come out during the round and as you've already learned, hope is just not a good game plan.

For those of you who play tournament golf this chapter is for you. The following stories, secrets, formulas, inspirations, tips and strategies are all written from a player who has been through it all and come out on the other side a better golfer because of it. Over the years I have documented my personal experiences, from the rounds of both tournament and practice golf, when confidence was high and nothing could go wrong to the slumps when my self-confidence was gone and nothing could go right. From those experiences I have gathered some winning ways to help you stay focused and motivated for better and more consistent performances in your pursuit to play scratch golf.

ON FOCUS

There are so many factors, many of which are out of your control, that determine what may happen during a shot or within a round of golf. Your focus is one factor that you can and must control during your round. Try my I.P.D.E. Formula to help you stay focused on every shot and try using mental triggers to go into a super state of focus every round.

I= IDENTIFY

Identify is the first and most important part of the formula because before you strike the ball or even take a club out of your bag, you must identify certain key factors. Your ability to identify just three factors will greatly improve your shot making.

The first factor to identify is the exact distance to the pin. You see it all the time on TV, caddies walking off yardages from ground markers so that they can give the exact yardage to the pro. Once you know the exact yardage you can get an idea started in your head as to which club you might use if indeed you know your perfect yardages of each club. Notice I said get an idea started as to which club you might use and that is because you still shouldn't pull a club from your bag until you have identified the other two factors necessary to hit a perfect shot.

The second factor you must identify is the lie. Every lie is different and every lie effects how the ball will jump off your clubface. Take the rough for example: the ball could be sitting on top of the grass, halfway down or settled deep at the bottom. Each will react differently and all three will react differently then a ball that lies in the fairway. Fairway lies are not all the same either and can be tight, sitting up, sitting down, on a slope or in a divot. Again each will react differently and your ability to identify what the lie will do to the flight of your ball is crucial in picking your club.

The last factor to identify before pulling a club from your bag is wind and weather. Is the wind into your face, behind you, cross to the right, cross to the left or swirling? Weather affects your distance and your ball flight and must always be considered before hitting your shot.

P= PREDICT

Once you have identified the three main factors and considered a club you want to use then you must look into the future and try to predict how the ball will fly through the air and how it will roll once it lands on the green or if on a par 5-hole, once it lands in the fairway. If you know the club you are going to play then you should know from your rang practice: the ball's spin, flight path and landing speed, which allows you to then predict how it will fly and bounce. If you have predicted properly then you can begin the next part of the formula.

D= DETERMINE

If you have identified and predicted properly then you can now search your arsenal of shots and determine which shot you will use. You probably already had a good idea of what shot you would try after identifying the three key factors but by going through the entire formula in order you make sure there isn't anything you may have left out in trying to hit the perfect shot. Once you have determined your shot to be played you can now act out and complete the formula.

E=EXECUTE

The ability to execute the chosen shot with the chosen club is of course what separates the professional players from the amateur players. Once you have determined the best shot to use you must be able to then execute it. And that is why a golfer must practice over and over again all the possible shots so that when a particular shot arises it is as comfortable to execute as an old pair of shoes; even under the most pressure-filled situations. Even the simplest of shots can become very difficult to execute if there is the added pressure of say a dollar bet of a Sunday game, a club championship or a U S Open trophy on the line. Let's look at a couple of examples:

Tiger Woods, playing in the 2005 Masters, had just missed the green on the par-3 16th hole and left himself with a very difficult chip. Most of those watching and the announcers in the booth all gave Tiger about a twenty percent chance to even get the ball inside his competitor's ball, which was about three feet from the cup. Tiger on the other hand is the best at using the I.P.D.E. formula I have ever seen. He identifies things that most golfers just don't see and has a great sense for predicting the future. On this particular shot he determined that his ball, if chipped to the top left of the green some twenty-five feet from the cup, would roll back down the slope and break towards the cup. He picked a spot on the green where he wanted to land the ball and determined the speed needed to get the ball rolling and then executed it perfectly. So perfectly in fact, that his ball rolled into the cup on its final revolution.

Jack Nicklaus was playing the Masters tournament in 1986 and making a charge on the back nine on Sunday. He was putting for birdie and the outright lead on the 17th hole and had a tricky downhill breaking putt. He went through the I.P.D.E. formula and identified that the putt was going to break back towards Rae's Creek as the ball neared the hole. He predicted the path the ball would roll, determined the speed needed to keep it on-line and then executed one of the most pressure-filled putts of all-time.

Both examples start with the number one element in the equation, identify and end with perfect execution. The great ones do it because they practice doing it each and every day. No it needs to be an every time occurrence, a habit, a routine and a way of life.

USE TRIGGERS TO GET IN THE ZONE

Golf is a game that requires you to maintain a certain level of focus if you want to succeed. Most unforced errors happen because of a loss of or reduced level of, focus. Your job as a player is to eliminate the unforced errors that can occur in a round by maintaining your focus from the first tee shot until the last putt. But even then that does not garuntee you a victory because, there are numerous times during a round when you need to be able to raise your normal level of focus and go into a super state of mental focus in order to achieve a desired outcome. This super state of mental focus is most commonly known in sports as the zone. The zone is such a high level of focus that no one can stay in it for an entire round, although the best golfers of the world, Tiger, Vjay, Phil and all the rest have learned how to put themselves in it and then stay in it much longer than the average player. So how do you raise your level of focus and get yourself into the zone more often in a round? The secret is to use mental triggers.

Mental triggers are physical, visual or vocal keys that trigger your mind into a super state of focus. An example of a physical trigger, and one that everyone can use, is when you immediately stand up after sitting down in the golf cart. The trigger is for you to believe the very next shot becomes the most important shot of the round. You are reminded to think this way every time you stand from sitting, a physical movement that you can use to trigger your mind into a super state of focus. Also, in the putting chapter you may recall the mental trigger of wiping the putter face, which is a physical trigger that I use to mentally heat up the putter to make more putts. Simply pulling a club from your bag can be the physical trigger that puts you into the zone. Any physical movement that is easy to remember and done often in the round would be good to use.

VOCAL TRIGGER: Let's say you are playing in your normal Sunday foursome and about to hit your tee shot on a tough par-5 dogleg with water bordering the entire right side of the fairway. One of the guys in your foursome, probably the jokester of the group, can't help but comment to you, "Hey don't bite off too much or you'll be swimming with the fishes." That vocal comment is your trigger to put yourself into a super state of mental focus. A focus that continues not only for that first tee shot to avoid the water but also for every shot you hit the entire hole. After you birdie or settle for a routine par on the hole, see if the jokester has any more comments for you to trigger off of while you play.

VISUAL TRIGGER: Let's say you just nailed a drive on a long par four that rolls down the middle of the fairway but comes to rest in a sandy old divot. An unlucky break, right? Wrong! When you approach your ball and first look down at what most golfers would be horrified by seeing, just smile. Because that bad lie is your visual trigger to go once again into a super state of mental focus for the rest of the hole. The announcer's in the booth or the player's playing along with you will all sympathize at your misfortune, or not, that is until your next shot lands to within ten feet of the flag. Think of all bad lies as an opportunity to showcase your talent and not as unlucky breaks.

Now you might say that you should be in a super state of mental focus anyway when playing any serious round of golf. And I agree that you should. But again, for the amateur golfer and even the seasoned tournament player that is not as easy it sounds. That is why it's good to have mental triggers throughout your round to help remind you or encourage you to go into that state of super focus. It's common knowledge that even Tiger uses mental triggers to keep himself in THE ZONE, during a tournament.

ON GAME DAY

The great champions of golf all have a common bond; they all know how to bring out their best performance on game day. Bringing out your best performance on game day is what matters most to the accomplished player. A week's worth of bad practices won't matter much if on game day you are performing your best. The professional players know that a poor performance means a smaller paycheck and a plane ticket home, so when a good performance happens you better believe me they remember exactly what they did before stepping on the first tee that day. Some players will develop wacky rituals and superstitions from a great performance day while others simply try and stick to a consistent routine. Your game day routine needs to begin well before you ever step onto the first tee and include a good warm-up.

It is important to make sure your body is ready to play and that you physically feel as good as you can. Quite often the physical side of the routine begins before you arrive at the golf course. Keep in mind it is possible that this may even start the night before. Consistency is critical to so many parts of golf and your warm up routine shouldn't vary. Your sleeping habits should remain the same meaning if you are used to going to bed at 11pm then you should go to bed at 11pm the night before your round. If you are used to waking up at 7am then assuming your tee time isn't too close to 7am, you should wake up at 7am. Your eating habits are included in your physical pre-game routine. If you don't typically eat spicy foods you will want to refrain from a spicy Mexican delight the night before an important round. If you are a big breakfast eater, allow yourself time to eat a big breakfast. Don't deviate from what you normally do and if you find that what you normally do doesn't leave you feeling your best you may want to consider changing what you normally do.

Arrive at the golf course with more than enough time to spare. One of the worst things you can do to yourself is to create a situation of feeling rushed or anxious. If you are early have a plan to combat the extra time. Bring a dozen golf balls with a sharpie marker and spend time marking an extra dozen for the day, take a walk through the clubhouse, or walk around the grounds gaining a feel of the event. If you get there so far before you are ready to begin your warm up remind yourself that your alternative could be a feeling of anxiety and distraction.

Mentally you need to spend time visualizing the shots you are expecting to hit that day. This can be done anytime prior to your round. Many players fall asleep the night before playing the course in their head, others begin to think about the shots on the car ride to the course and continue the process throughout their warm up. The key to the mental part of your routine is finding a way to help you feel comfortable and at ease with yourself on the day of the round. Doing the same thing every time puts you in a comfort zone so find what ever it is works for you and plan to duplicate it every time. Here is a sample of an effective warm up routine for a 9am tee time that allows for a good physical and mental warm-up.

7:00am

Arrive at the course and walk around, stretch and get out the kinks from the ride. Find a place to put your shoes on, go to the restroom, put sunscreen on, and any other pre-round maintenance you might have and be sure to wash the sunscreen off your hands.

7:20am

Get your clubs on a cart or out of your car. Use your wedge to do some more light stretching and begin limbering up your back, neck, shoulders, arms, and legs.

7:30am

Arrive at the putting green. Begin by hitting ten 3-footers. Follow that with ten 4-footers and then ten five 5-footers. Now work on getting the speed of the greens by putting back and forth from one fringe to the other. Your goal in the putting warm up is not only to get a feel for the speed of the greens, but also to begin hearing putts drop in the hole and getting used to making putts. It's a great way to start your warm up, both physically and mentally. Making a putt is how you start your day on the course and it will be how you end your day as well.

7:42am

Use your favorite chipping club to chip five shots from a good lie. Slowly back up and chip a total of 15 shots.

7:50am

Stretch out again on the range tee. Make sure you include your back, legs, arms, and shoulders. You should have a stretching routine that properly prepares you for a round that takes about 10 minutes. If you need additional stretching time you need to plan for it.

8:00am

Start your swinging with a weighted club, or two clubs at once. When you are loose move to your shortest wedge. Hit 5 of each of your wedges making the effort to swing no more than 75% speed on any one swing.

Next, hit five 8 irons, then three 6 irons, then three 4 irons. By this time you have made around thirty full swings depending on how many wedges you carry.

8:17am

Time to hit your long clubs. You are loose and should be ready to make some full swings so grab your longest iron or hybrid that you might use for a tee shot. Hit two shots picking a specific target. If you know you are going to use the club off of a tee that day, visualize the shot and then execute it. Do the same with your fairway woods, hitting two of each, and then with the driver. Hit five drivers in all, with each one visualizing a particular tee shot for the day. The final driver hit the tee shot you intend to hit off the first tee.

8:25am

Finish your warm up by hitting seven more wedges the distance you consider your favorite distance. This should be that distance you will try to leave yourself whenever possible during your round.

8:32am

Hit 6 basic bunkers shots from a flat, perfect lie. Hit one from a plugged lie, and one from a downhill lie.

8:40am

Hit five more 4-foot putts followed by three 3 footers.

8:50am

Arrive at the tee for your 9:00am tee time and make sure your clubs arrive with you.

I was playing the 2007 Mid-Amateur and had a tee time of 8am. As I stood on the tee swinging my club, the other player I was paired with that day came running up to the tee box from the range but without his clubs. When the PGA official called our starting time he asked the other player where his clubs were. The player pointed to his caddy who was walking up with the clubs but about 25yards away from the tee box. The official immediately accessed the player with a 2 stroke penalty claiming that the rules state that you must have a club and ball in hand when your tee time is called. There was a lot of yelling by the player and a discussion with the other officials but the penalty remained and before the player had ever hit a ball he was 2 over.

Remember to leave time to transport from different areas of the practice facility. You should never be in a hurry and you should never be running up to the first tee always be taking your time between everything you do. Tell yourself that you are going to go through your pre-game routine at a comfortable, smooth pace and this feel is going to run over into your round.

Every routine is going to be different. What is important is that you tailor one that works for you and then stick to it every time you play. This is your chance to get ready to play, use it to prepare to play the best round of your life.

If you're not just a little bit nervous before a match, you probably don't have the expectations of yourself that you should have.

— Hale Irwin

ON PRESSURE

➲ Pressure is a part of every athletes life, so embrace it, make it yours. If you can control it, you will thrive on it and you will succeed!

➲ Never use the pressure from others as an excuse for losing. The only reason there is any outside pressure is because you have a chance to do something big. Remember that other's expectations of you are not why you're playing anyway.

➲ Realize pressure situations and learn to love them. You want to have the attitude that: the more pressure there is, the better you will play.

➲ Pressure from within usually comes about when you know you haven't properly prepared for the performance at hand.

➲ Practice playing rounds under pressure. Give your opponent a 3 stroke lead and see if you can win.

➲ Don't pretend there is no pressure. Three-foot putts, tight fairways, thick rough, long carries over water and fast greens are all full of pressure and denying it won't help you to play better.

➲ To relieve pressure, don't be so concerned with winning or losing. Be more concerned with your performance. If it is good then you will win.

➲ Remember that all the other golfers in the tournament feel pressure. They are playing the same course in the same conditions, so a tough hole for you is a tough hole for them.

ON SUCCESS

BELIEF IN YOURSELF AND YOUR TALENT (X) DISCIPLINED HARD WORK (+) TAKING ADVANTAGE OF OPPORTUNITIES = SUCCESS

The first ingredient of the formula, Belief in yourself and your talent, is without a doubt the most important. Without it, you have no chance of lowering your handicap or ever becoming a tour professional. The one thing that all champions have is a deep belief that they can win no matter what the odds. They feel that there is nothing that they can't accomplish. They will go into each round, match, race, game or whatever the competition, expecting to out perform their opponents each and every time and never doubt their offensive or defensive strategies. They believe inside that their talent, in the end, is far greater then that of their opponents. Having that kind of inner confidence is what separates the contenders from the pretenders. Opponents and spectators will know by your performance just how confident a golfer you really are on the inside. They'll begin to refer to you as a true competitor, a fighter, a someone with tremendous desire and hopefully, eventually, a champion. Belief in yourself will definitely start you on your climb but it will take the discipline to work hard every day to get you to the top.

I've seen many a talented golfers reach the fullness of their talent and then fall by the wayside because they weren't willing to work hard everyday to improve upon what talents they were given. Self-discipline is something that everyone has come across in their lives at some point or another, whether or not they were able or willing to practice it is another story. If you have the self-discipline to work hard then you can take your talent a lot further then someone who has no self-discipline with exceptional talent. If you have the belief in yourself and you work hard then to complete the formula you must take advantage of opportunities.

When you are on the course and you hit a poor shot that leaves you with a chance to recover then you must take advantage. If your playing in a match play tournament and your opponent misses a sure gimmie then you must take advantage. If you are the first alternate to get into a tournament and someone calls in sick then you must be ready to play and take advantage of the situation. There are numerous stories throughout history of talented people who did not succeed because they weren't ready to take advantage of an opportunity once it presented itself, don't let that happen to you.

ON STRATEGY

All that practicing on your swing technique, short game skills, long game, putting, off course training and mental game will pay dividends for you in the long run but to lower your handicap the fastest and become a scratch golfer sooner you must learn how to score. To score you must strategize and tactically attack the golf course with your current game. The top tour players are master tacticians and never hit a shot without properly thinking out the end results both good and bad. To them every shot is as important as the one before it and if they can't pull off a shot successfully then they have learned to take out the risk so as not to turn a possible bogey into a disaster. Just as a top tennis player will think one or two shots ahead in a rally so does a professional golfer plan ahead and try to predict all possible outcomes of a shot. To better understand course strategy, here is an example of the multiple-shot mistake, which can turn a good round into a disaster.

On my first hole at the Honda Classic Qualifier, I pull-hooked my tee shot through the woods on the left and into a small creek. I had to take a penalty drop that left me 220 yards from the hole. After taking the drop I noticed there was an opening in the trees that followed the creek all the way up to the slightly elevated green. I was lying 2 hitting 3 so my thinking was if I chipped out and then hit on the green and two putted I would get a double bogey, a score that was not going to help me qualify. But, and this is where the amateur in me really showed through, if I were to hit a high cut following the creek line up to and onto the green then I could possibly one-putt and save par. So, I tried it! I came up well short of the green, landing in some high grass on the wrong side of the creek just before the green. Then to make matters worse, I tried a ridiculous flop shot out of the high grass that landed in the middle of the creek. I had to drop again but did manage to hit my next shot onto the green although I was unconscious of it because at this point I was so nervous about holding everyone up that I couldn't think straight. I three-putted of course and had to ask my father what I had gotten on the hole. " 9," he said. I tried to write it down but my hands were shaking too much.

This scenario of making one mistake after another happens to amateur golfers all the time. They try to hit the glory-shot instead of the safe or smart shot, which only brings in more risk, more trouble and more penalties. Bringing in more risk, instead of limiting the risk, is simply poor course management. You will rarely see a tour pro trying to hit a wood or long iron out of heavy rough or through a small gap in the trees and especially not to an elevated green, because those types of multiple-shot mistakes are round killers. The moral of the story is when practicing course strategies think, safe and smart. Safe for landing areas and approach shots and smart for club selections and strategies.

ON PAR-3 HOLES

Par-3 holes are what I call, one-shot-drama holes because let's face it, it's all about the tee shot. Think about it, you step on to the tee and in one swing you can ruin a great score, set yourself up for an easy par or end up buying drinks for everyone at the club by sinking a hole-in-one. That's what makes par-3 holes so great to watch on TV and that's what makes them so pressure-filled to play.

Par-3 holes are always surrounded or guarded by all sorts of stroke stealing trouble and any errant tee shot is sure to find that trouble, whether it's a bunker, thick rough, trees, out-of-bounds or water. The penalties and strokes can add up fast and that's why YOU MUST ALWAYS play to par the par-3 holes. Consider a birdie like stealing one stroke. Par must be had on these holes to preserve a good round so if that means hitting away from the flag to the fat part of the green to take the trouble out of play then by all means do it.

PAR-3 STRATEGIES

OVER WATER — When the green is fronted by water you must take short out of play. If the yardage is normally a 6-iron for you then consider, no definitely, take out the 5-iron. With the extra club you will swing easier at the ball and hit a better shot. If you think it's too much club you can still choke down and still clear the water, taking short out of play.

TROUBLE LEFT — If the green has trouble left then right is right. Aim at the flag or center of the green and play a cut shot. If the shot cuts as you plan then you will be putting from the right of the hole. If the shot doesn't cut then you're right at the flag or in the center of the green but you've taken left out of play.

TROUBLE RIGHT — If the green has trouble right then left is your play. If you can play a draw then aim at the flag or center of the green and hit the draw. If your ball doesn't draw then you're on the flagstick or in the center of the green and you've still taken the trouble out of play.

TROUBLE LONG — If the trouble is behind the green then short is the play. Be sure to check the wind in this situation because you don't want your perfectly hit iron sailing over the green.

SURROUNDED — When you think of par-3 holes that are surrounded by water, I'm sure number 17 at Sawgrass comes to mind. Every golfer in the world wants a chance at this famous hole. So what's the strategy when the green is surrounded by trouble? You either need to come in high and soft or with plenty of spin. First, always tee the ball up. Teeing up the ball will help you hit it high or spin the ball better. Next get in your hands, your favorite club nearest the yardage of the hole. It might not be the perfect club for the yardage but it's the club that you trust the most and with trouble all around the green, trust is what you need more than anything to hit the green.

ON PAR-5 HOLES

GO BIG OR GO HOME! You've all heard this before that hitting a big drive is the key to going low on the par-5 holes, especially if it's a short or dogleg par-5. If you can cut off some major real estate with the tee shot then pulling out the driver is a calculated risk worth taking.. Most all tour players look at par-5's as scoring holes and the attitude of "birdie or better" is how you should approach these holes as well when you are swinging your best. The thing to consider most on all par-5's is the risk/reward factor. Unlike the par-3's and par-4's, the par 5's all have some sort of risk/reward opportunity designed into them. They also have the ample length to save you if that risk/reward shot happens to go offline. Most often it's the second shot from 200-265 yards out that is the risk/reward shot but it can also be the tee shot, which is the risk/reward shot because a long tee shot often sets up an easier second shot. What this tells you is that if you want to start scoring better on the par-5's then you need to work on all your long clubs: driver, long irons, hybrids and fairway woods to be able to carry the distances needed to go big or go home.

PLAN AHEAD FOR A 3 SHOT HOLE! When facing a par-5 hole that has either water crossing the fairway, dangerous penalty areas surrounding the green or is playing into the wind it is smart to take out the urge to go for it in two while still on the tee box. Leave the driver in the bag in other words and pull out the 3-wood or even a hybrid club for your first shot. That way you won't hit your first shot into the possible go-zone and be tempted to go for it once you get up to your ball. By laying back you can now dissect the hole and position your second shot into an area of the fairway that favors your desired yardage. A wedge in your hands on the third shot usually allows you to go flag hunting and have a make able birdie putt or who knows, you could still hole out for eagle. For most amateur players this is the strategy of choice because hitting the green in two shots is usually out of reach anyway. What this means is that if you what to score better on the par-5's then you need to work on your shots from 120 yards and in. That means your short irons: 9 iron, pitching wedge, lob wedge and sand wedge all need to be precise.

PRACTICE TO BE IN THE LAST GROUP

Want a great way to prepare your game for being in the final group on Sunday? Practice in the late afternoons! The course is a much different animal late in the day then it is early in the morning. The key factors effected late in the day are: the wind blows more in the afternoons, the greens have grown and become littered with spike marks, there are different shadows on the course due to the sun angle and the crowd watching is always bigger and louder. OK, so there might not be the crowd factor when you play practice rounds but the other factors mentioned are definitely different late in the day.

ON HITTING MORE GREENS
Know Your Yardages

The key to hitting more greens is knowing how far you can carry each of your clubs. In other words you must know your yardages in order to produce a shot that is needed to get over and avoid any greenside trouble. Every hole is designed so that as you look towards the flags you see the trouble that lies ahead of you. This visual intimidation is a holes last line of defense to hopefully deter you from taking dead aim at the flag. How do you conquer that intimidation? Know and be confident in every clubs yardage.

Tour players rarely come up short when attacking greens and would rather error on the long then become a sucker to the holes front defense. That's why they carry three wedges if not four to fill in the yardage gaps from 130 yards and in, the scoring yards. They never want to have to hit a perfect shot with any club just to get to the green. You can't garuntee your ball landing exactly where you plan on hitting it or hope it might make it to the flag. Trying to hit the perfect shot into a green is for days when your game is on fire and not a habit you want to practice regularly. Instead know your yardages so that you can take a club that gives you plenty of distance and if you are in-between yardages practice taking too much club so that you don't error on the short side.

ON UNEVEN LIES

When you watch The Masters tournament every year and see those remarkable shots, what you don't always see, is the multitude of un-even lies that the pros have to deal with on their shots because of the extreme elevation changes of the course. Uneven lies can cause every golfer to rethink their shot choice because of the fact that you are in a situation that is out of your comfort zone. Understanding the ball flight rules and how they relate to uneven lies can be a huge source of confidence.

In general every type of lie has a rule in the world of physics that tell you what the ball will do if everything else in your swing remains status quo. This can be a big IF because so often a funky lie will subconscious-ly tell you to manipulate the club to compensate for the uneven lie. This is a dangerous thing to attempt so avoid trying to manufacture a shot in these cases. Take a look at these ball flight rules and give them a try during practice to see how they relate to your golf swing.

Ball Below Your Feet

A general rule for all uneven lies is that you never fight gravity. For the lie that has the ball below your feet don't sit back on your heels and try to lean away from the ball. Instead lean with the hill and get to where you feel you are almost looking on top of the ball. Set up with a wider than normal stance to assist in balance during the swing.

The ball-flight rule for the ball below your feet says your ball will move from left to right caused by the side-spin that is created when a square swing makes contact on a consistent plane. The angle of the hill will create a slightly open club face, which will cause the left-to-right spin. The amateur tendency with this shot is to hit it "thin" because the feel-ing is to pull away from the ball.

Ball Above Your Feet

Set up stable and wide for this shot. You don't want to lean into the hill when the ball is above your feet, instead you will stand slightly closer to the ball and lean away from the ball. This lie naturally flattens your swing causing the tendency to pull the shot and also putting a right-to-left, hook-spin on the ball. Be sure to play for your ball to come out to the left if you find yourself in this situation. The tendency for this shot is to hit is fat because the hill causes you to feel it necessary to lean into the shot, which isn't the case.

Downhill Lie

If you find yourself hitting down a hill you have a couple of tendencies to keep in mind. First, you are going to have to work hard to stay behind the ball. Secondly, the ball is going to come off the club at a much lower trajectory than what you are used to.

Set up to the ball with a narrow stance relative to what you normally would for the club you are hitting. Focus on keeping your lower body as still as you can to avoid a lateral slide through the impact position. Play the ball towards the back of your stance creating a situation where you will have impact earlier in the swing thus taking loft off the shot and producing a stronger shot.

The ball flight rules for the downhill lie say that the ball will have the tendency to go right slightly so you should allow for a 10-15% push, again assuming everything else is status quo. The ball will also come out much lower and most likely travel 10-15% further depending on the slope of the hill you are hitting from.

Uphill Lie

The uphill lie ball flight rule says the ball will have the tendency to pull left. Again, don't fight the hill. Let your shoulders match the slope of the hill at the address position and work hard to return them to that same position at impact. The ball will also come out higher than normal thus taking distance off the shot.

To play this shot take a wider than normal stance to help restrict lower body movement. As you take your backswing you should feel like you are extending the arms and the club head down the hill away from the ball. This will allow you to return to the ball on a flatter plane allowing a sweeping of the ball. It is important not to dig the club into the ground, you can't move the hill in most cases. Work hard to transfer your weight during the swing because if you don't you will pull the ball even more than what you already are projected to.

ON A PLAYER'S LIFE

☞ Hit golf balls everyday to add the needed layers to your swing. A seven-layer cake without the layers is a pancake.

☞ Avoid those who do not understand or believe in your goals and dreams.

☞ Find a good coach as inspiration, technique, success, strategy and desire rub off.

☞ When you're having a bad practice day, give yourself a break. Remember Rome wasn't built in a day.

☞ Do something positive everyday to advance your game, your character, your goals or your knowledge.

☞ Enjoy the development years of your game because it's those years and not the big finish that makes a life.

☞ Set high goals for yourself and then attach deadlines to achieving each one.

☞ After a bad round, remember, there's always tomorrow for dreams to come true.

☞ Play more tournaments if you want more victories.

☞ Don't rush your game. Go slow and make sure you are ready.

☞ Play for yourself. Not for your parents, your coaches or anyone else.

☞ Love the game not the money or the fame. Money can be earned a lot easier and those who have fame live their lives in the fear of losing it.

☞ Never celebrate a bad win!

☞ Maintain the long vision and don't be discouraged by the shortcomings along the way.

☞ Accept responsibility for your failures. Learn from them and then move on.

☞ Don't make excuses or blame anyone or anything else when you play bad.

☞ Don't be quick to believe all those press releases and people talking about your talent. Desire and hard work may have had more to do with it.

☞ Never speak of your victories or achievements. If others speak fine, it will be heard tenfold.

☞ There is pleasure and pain in every situation. Be the optimist.

☞ Always play to win against par.

☞ Stop repeating losing patterns, as consistency in failure is no virtue.

☞ Do not put any golfer on a pedestal. It dwarfs you and gains you nothing.

☞ Run your own race. Stay focused on your goals and dreams.

☞ Never be satisfied in results that come up just short of the goal. In every tournament there is only one winner.

☞ When you are out played give credit where credit is due.

☞ Dream that you can, then pursue that dream everyday with all your heart.

☞ Never forget why you started playing golf— Because it's Fun!

ON ACHIEVEING YOUR DREAMS

⯈ Dream that you can! — Before you can achieve anything you have to Dream it first. See yourself holding up the US Open trophy high over your head while a packed crowd gives you a standing ovation for your great performance. Now that you've dreamed it, you need to set goals along the way to achieving it.

⯈ Put your goals down on paper and sign it—This is your contract with yourself to do whatever it takes to achieve those goals.

⯈ Once you achieve a goal check it off your list—When a goal is achieved check it off your list and replace it with another goal that is on your path towards your dream. If your goal is to add ten yards to your driver and you do it then give yourself an award for your achievement and then move on to the next goal or try to improve upon the goal you have just achieved.

⯈ Don't set goals you can't achieve—If your list of goals doesn't have any checks on it after 6 months, then maybe you set goals that are unrealistic of your ability. Reassess your goals and make sure you have some goals that you can achieve in: 1 month, 3 months, 6 months, 1 year, 3 years and lifetime.

⯈ Find out what drives you—People that accomplish great things are driven. They have a fire within them that keeps them focused on their goals. What is it that drives you? Remember that your goals are just that, your goals. To be truly driven you must play for yourself and not for anyone else's expectations of you. Playing to please others is a fire that is easily extinguished. Playing for you is a fire that never burns out!

⯈ Discipline yourself—You won't accomplish any of your goals or get far down the path of your dream if you don't have self-discipline. Being able to say no to that candy bar and yes to ten more crunches is a key ingredient to what I call—Dream Achieving.

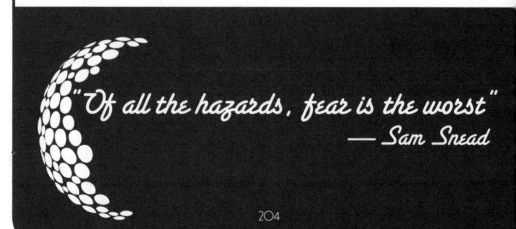

"Of all the hazards, fear is the worst"
— Sam Snead

CHAPTER

9

The Shot Secrets

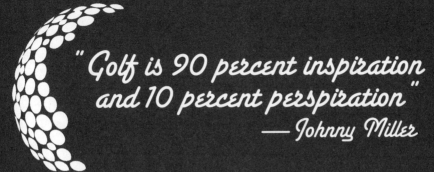

"Golf is 90 percent inspiration and 10 percent perspiration"
— Johnny Miller

The High Cut

The secret to the High Cut shot is the swing path and shoulder angle at the impact position. The steeper you can make your shoulder angle by keeping your right shoulder down and behind the ball the higher the shot will travel. By changing your swing path to a more outside-in path you will have a slightly open club face at impact causing the left to right spin and the cut shot. The more open the club face, the more the ball will cut and the steeper your shoulder angle the higher the trajectory.

The Tiger Stinger

The "Tiger Stinger" is a shot that requires great physical strength, flexibility, and timing. The stinger shot moves gradually from left to right and is a controlled, low trajectory, fade. The club must be coming at the ball from a steep, outside-in swing path. The secret to the shot is the hands and arms must "hold on" to the club to produce a de-lofted face and at the same time a slightly open face. Too much of either can cause a wayward shot and leave you in trouble so make sure you practice this one before you use it.

The Controlled Fade

Working the ball left to right is the safest shot in golf. When you need to get one in the fairway this is a great shot to have in your arsenal. The secret to the controlled fade is to hit the shot by "controlling" your clubface through the impact position. Don't change your swing path on this shot since you are only working the ball a minimal amount. Allowing your hands to hold the face slightly open through the impact zone will cause a slight left-to-right ball flight. Make sure you aim just a little to the left to allow for the fade!

The 30 Yard Hook

The secret to this shot is the angle of the clubface at impact. To produce a massive hook shut the clubface at address pointing to the target. Align your body far enough to the right to allow for the hook you are trying to generate. Make your swing "rounder" than normal to accentuate the hook. Keep in mind a ball in the rough won't hook as much as a ball from a clean lie.

Out of a Divot

Hitting out of a divot is not as difficult as it may sound. The secret is to play the ball back in your stance about two inches ensuring that you hit down on the ball and strike the golf ball first. The tendency of this shot will be for the ball to come out traveling left-to-right. Putting the ball back in the stance helps to hit with a descending blow but it will also keep the clubface from squaring completely therefore producing a slight fade.

Knock Down

The knock down shot is specific to controlling the trajectory of a shot. Most often you would use this shot when hitting into a headwind or even hitting downwind in an effort to keep the wind from affecting the distance of the shot. The secret is to use two clubs more than you would use under normal conditions and then choke down to make it the same length of the club you would normally use. For example: if a 9-iron would be your play under normal conditions, you would use your 7-iron and choke down to make it the same length as your 9-iron. Play the ball off your left heel for this shot. Controlling the angle of the clubface at impact is critical to pulling this shot off. Use an abbreviated backswing and be aggressive on your downswing holding the face of the club well past impact. The less curve and spin on the ball the better, getting the club head on the target line early and keeping it there well past the ball will produce the best results.

The Hybrid Chip

Using your hybrid to play a chip shot is a great advantage when you face a thick lie or when you have to clip one over an irrigation head very close to the green. You may also use a hybrid when you have a steep embankment to chip up or just an extremely tight lie close to the green. The hybrid chip is effective because the bulky head of the club both in size and weight helps to propel the club head with enough acceleration to ensure effective results. The secret is to grip it like your putter and then choke down all the way to the shaft. Use the same stroke you would for a putt and let the loft of the club lift the ball through, over, or around the trouble.

The Toe Putt

If you have played golf long enough you have encountered a putt that sits on top of a steep slope and the hole is cut at the bottom of the hill. You look at the putt and know you just need to get it started for it to hopefully stop somewhere near the hole. Using the toe end of the putter is an effective way to "deaden" the shot and control the speed. You don't want to hit the putt squarely on the sweet spot and risk getting the putt started much too fast. The secret is to line the putt up just off the outside edge of the putter head and trust the same stroke that you always make.

Zip It Back Wedge

Keep in mind there is never a time you need to spin back a wedge shot but there are certain situations where using this approach may be a higher percentage shot than other options. The secret to this shot is that you make crisp, solid contact and that you are very aggressive through impact. Your hands have to work together with your body to insure the proper angle of attack is achieved and the correct amount of rotation is produced on the downswing. Eliminate all lateral movement to successfully accomplish this most difficult shot. Remember, the one thing you must achieve to execute this shot to precision is solid contact.

Put On The Brakes Pitch Shot

One of the prettiest shots in golf when you execute it to perfection is the two-bounce and stop pitch shot. This shot is a little about technique and more about touch. In order to get your ball to spin enough to stop from relatively short distances, takes great control of the clubface and the willingness to be very aggressive. Pick the club up abruptly with your hands hinging immediately, once at the top of the backswing hold your hands until your arms, shoulders, and chest pull them down. Let the rotation of your body drive the club head down on the ball making a steep, descending blow holding your hands through impact. Try to get the feeling that the ball will touch each one of the grooves on the club face at some point during the shot, each groove will provide more spin, if you miss one you'll miss the spin. Let your hands be soft throughout the shot especially at impact. The secret is to have the correct speed of your body working together with your soft hands to produce the spin.

Chunk And Run Bunker Shot

As with any bunker shot you cannot expect to use finesse with this shot. The combination of keeping spin off the shot and making sure the ball stays in the air the correct distance is what will produce the best result for this shot. The secret to keeping spin off the ball is hitting the sand well behind the ball. To ensure the ball flying the right distance you mustn't hit too far behind the ball. Address the ball with a slightly closed clubface unless you need to get the ball in the air quickly. Put the ball back in your stance and lean towards the target placing 75% of your weight on the left side. Lift the club with your arms and hands creating a steep angle. Drive the club down from that steep angle entering the sand far enough behind the ball so that the sand between the clubface and the ball will keep the ball from spinning. The ball should come out with a low trajectory, land on the green and roll at least the same distance it was in the air. This is one of the most difficult shots in golf and requires a great deal of practice before you try it in play.

The 40—yard Flopper

The Flopper from 40-yards would be a necessity when you are faced with a tree between you and the green that you have to go over and you have a very small area of the green to stop the ball. The only way you can pull this shot off is if you have a great lie, without it you better find a different shot to play. The secret to hitting this shot is to open the club face as much as you can, widen your stance more than twice the width of your regular stance and set up open to the target. This is not a finesse shot. You must swing at this with great confidence and tremendous aggression. Your ability to hold the angle of the clubface while swinging with great force will determine how well you execute your shot. If you want the shot to go further you need to either swing harder, or decrease the loft slightly.

The Low Draw

The low draw is a combination of two shot characteristics that both depend on the angle of the clubface at impact. Controlling the clubface at impact means you must have good control over the rest of the swing and then manipulate the hands through the hitting zone. Your set up will have your alignment out to the right and the ball placed in the back of your stance. Getting your ball to draw requires a slightly closed clubface at impact, so set your clubface closed at address. The secret is placing the ball back in your stance so it feels like you are dragging the club through impact, which will keep the ball low. Your arms and shoulders should follow what the rotation of the body is asking them to do. Practice with your ball position in different spots and the amount in which you close your club ace at address to change the trajectory and curve in the shot.

The Side— Spin Bunker Shot

Open your stance almost 45 degrees from the target line and set up to the shot very wide. The secret to this shot is making certain that your swing path is working distinctly from outside-in and coming across the ball at impact. The distance you hit behind the ball will determine the amount of spin placed on the ball. The outside-in swing path will create the side-spin. Be sure to aim far enough to the left allowing for the spin to be effective.

The Low Slice

When you need to hit a low slicing shot your ability to execute the shot will depend on your ability to hold on to the club while laterally moving through the shot. This is one of the only times you are trying to move laterally during a shot. Place the ball off your left toe at address and be sure your hands are in front of the ball to help the feel of keeping the clubface closed. Align yourself to the left to prepare for the left-to-right curve of the ball but also to produce a outside-in swing path. The secrets to this shot is taking the club up outside the line and then, as you begin the downswing, allow the center of your torso to begin to slide forward gradually. By the time you reach the impact zone the middle of your torso should be holding on the rotation and your arms have lead your hands in front of the ball creating a hooded clubface that is also slightly open. The two characteristics combined will produce a low slice, one of the most difficult shots in golf.

In The Water… but only half way

When your ball is partially submerged in the water the rule of thumb says if half the ball is showing then you have a chance to play the ball. Hitting this shot is much like hitting a shot out of a plugged lie in a bunker. Open your stance to the target and hood the clubface at address.

You won't know exactly what the ground under the ball is like but you should be able to get an idea by feeling the firmness with your feet. The secret to this shot is to create a steep swing angle and hit abruptly down, slightly behind the ball. The ball will exit the water with no spin and will roll out once it lands. You must be aggressive with this shot to be certain you aren't left with the same shot again, or worse.

Split the Fairways

When stepping onto the tee box, you should always be looking for landing zones that continually take big numbers out of play. Water, bunkers, out-of-bounds and trees are all hazards that lay waiting your indecisive choice of strategy off the tee. Once you've identified the trouble try working your ball away from that trouble to a safe landing area. If there's a bunker on the right, aim to the edge of the right fairway slightly inside the bunker and play a draw that will curve your ball away from the bunker and out towards the middle of the fairway. If the trouble is on the left, aim at the left edge of the fairway and play a cut or fade shot. The secret is in aiming slightly outside the bunker instead of at the bunker as that will save you if you do happen to hit the ball straight.

Flipped over Wedge

This is a shot that you may need if your ball ever comes to rest next to a tree or bush and you can't swing a club from your normal side. If you are a righty then this is a time when you probably wish you had a lefty's club in your bag. The solution is to grab your wedge, flip it over and swing it from your left side. Tennis players swing from both sides all the time and the flipped over wedge is simply a backhand used in tennis. The secret to this shot is to use a club with loft like your wedge and then don't over do it. All you want to do is drop the club down into the back of the ball. You don't normally swing from this side but you do know how to swing a club so apply your fundamentals to how a lefty would hold and swing a club and then hit it using a three-quarters swing.

NOTES

Golf

NOTES

NOTES

_____
_____
_____
_____
_____
_____
_____
_____
_____
_____
_____
_____
_____
_____
_____
_____
_____
_____
_____
_____
_____

Golf

NOTES

NOTES

Golf

NOTES

NOTES

Golf

NOTES

Index

Index